W9-AKY-920

IN SEARCH OF SEMIOTICS

IN SEARCH OF SEMIOTICS

David Sless

BARNES & NOBLE BOOKS
Totowa, New Jersey

© David Sless 1986
first published in the USA 1986 by
Barnes & Noble Books
81 Adams Drive
Totowa, New Jersey, 07512
Printed in Great Britain

Library of Congress Cataloging-in-Publication Data

Sless, David.
    In search of semiotics.

    Bibliography: p.
    Includes index.
    1. Semiotics. I. Title.
P99.S55 1986   001.51   86-14141
ISBN 0-389-20660-1

CONTENTS

To the memory of Ben Sless

PREFACE

Semiotics is far too important an enterprise to be left to semioticians. This book is not written for them. I have written this book for everyone with an interest in our wondrous capacity to create meaning and understanding.

Over the last 15 years, since I began to take a serious interest in semiotics, I have met many intelligent and thoughtful people who have turned to semiotics for illumination and deeper insight, only to be disappointed; obfuscation and esoteric jargon have rendered much of it unintelligible. Initial interest and enthusiasm quickly turned into cynicism, rejection, or — worse — a sense of intellectual inadequacy. For them I hope this book will rekindle interest.

For the reader approaching semiotics for the first time I hope this book will generate a passion for what I believe to be our most important capacity: creating and using messages.

A clear purpose has guided me in writing this book. I wanted from the start to build as simple a way of talking about semiotics as I could. I wanted very much to create a contrast to all the tortured prose that surrounded me. I don't know if I have succeeded. My doubt does not arise from a sense of modesty, false or otherwise. I am, as the readers of this book will discover, not given to trembling caution.

My uncertainty comes from semiotics itself. You will have to read this book to understand why. However, allow me to caution you about the *nature of understanding*, to prepare you for reading this book. Understanding is achieved when, for a moment, there are no more questions to ask. Understanding is the dead spot in our struggle for meaning: it is the momentary pause, the stillness before incomprehension continues; it is the brief relief from the doubt that is the norm. Thus understanding is a temporary state of closure. When we understand something we are effectively saying there is no more to ask, no more to question, all is revealed. But of course 'all' is never revealed and the sensation of certainty always passes.

If you are in search of final understanding, semiotics is not for you. But if you are in search of limits, interested in the edge of things and in the delicious savour of uncertainty, then semiotics will take you there.

Preface

This book is a record of my own search. I have tried to make it clear and coherent so that the arguments and ideas can be followed from point to point. I recommend the reader to progress through it in the sequence in which it is presented. I have tried to remove from my account all the traces of struggle and difficulty which attended my search.

The most difficult task for me was to clear some of the thicket and weed that had been planted by others who have taken the same route. I have tried where possible to plant a little mirth in the compost made from the uprooted vegetation. And as this is a book for people who are fascinated by our ways of making meaning I have indulged in a little play with metaphors along the way. I hope you will enjoy the journey.

ACKNOWLEDGEMENTS

I suspect that furious semiotic debates erupted while the paint was still wet on the walls of the caves at Lascaux. The echoes from those heated exchanges in the flickering light and long shadows have rumbled down the centuries. They have joined the sound of all the other voices which, on discovering semiosis, argued about its magical power and value. I have been arguing with people about the ideas which led to this book for only the last 15 years. Within such a scheme I have difficulty taking my own contribution too seriously.

Many of my contemporaries, locked into an obsession with the present, take themselves and their thinking very seriously. I have been unable to argue directly with them despite many attempts both public and private. They have a much stronger need than I to be correct, and they defend their views with all the conviction and isolation of zealots.

Yet this book is deeply indebted to their thinking. Without their voluminous writing and fashionable excesses this book would never have been written. It is against the endless elaboration that I have tried to construct my simple semiotics. It is against the obscurantism and tortured neologisms that I have tried to write clearly and simply. It is against the deep divisiveness of critical versus empirical approaches that I have tried to develop a unified approach. It is against the high seriousness that I have reacted with irreverence.

Doubtless within such an enterprise I will have misunderstood some important issues, misrepresented some ideas or failed to acknowledge some important contribution. I expect to be wrong about many things and I would welcome being corrected. I only hope that I will understand the criticisms when they are made.

While I will take the blame for all the faults for this book, the credit for any merit it may have must be widely distributed. As the reader will discover, I have little faith in the idea that a single communicator, however professional, can effectively get his message across and I have absolutely no faith in any practice based on such a silly idea, least of all my own. This book is the end result of the help, support and advice of family, friends and colleagues.

Foremost among these has been Ruth who has given all three —

help, support and advice — while coping with the many other aspects of our domestic life neglected by me over the long period during which this book evolved. Her unerring sense of style and incisive clarity of thought have guided the construction of every sentence in this book.

Anne Brewster edited all but the final two chapters and gave me many penetrating criticisms that helped me understand some of the problems of reading this book. Many of my colleagues at Flinders University read drafts of the early chapters and gave me useful criticisms and encouragement in the long struggle to write this book. They include Andrew Bear, Donald Brook, Doug Brown, Adrian Ceasar, John Harwood and Michael Meehan. My thanks also to Ken Baker for the illustration on page 56.

I would like to offer a special thanks to Syd Harrex. We seldom discussed the substance of the book but his constant friendship and acute sensitivity to the intellectual and ethical issues which framed my thinking helped me immeasurably.

I am very grateful to Flinders University which supported me while most of this book was written. In particular I would like to thank the Research and Outside Studies Committees for their direct support of this project.

Many of the arguments in this book were first tried out with Communication Studies and Visual Communication students at Flinders University. My thanks to them for their enthusiasm, patience and forebearance in the face of my idiosyncratic and annoying doubts about their strongly held convictions.

During 1978/9 I spent a period of study leave in England at Birmingham University Centre for Cultural Studies and at Aston University Applied Psychology, Information Research Unit. The curious combination of Cultural Studies and Visual Information Design coalesced in my mind to give me the first strong convictions that this book, an attempt to provide a unified approach, was possible. I would like to thank Stuart Hall who was then at Birmingham University and Ronald Easterby at Aston University for allowing me to participate in their seminars and research. I hope from their respective approaches they will find this book adequate thanks for their generosity.

I would like to thank Robyn Penman for her enthusiastic and critical support of my work over the last few months. The last chapters were written while the first chapters were being put into practice here in Canberra. Robyn shares with me a dedicated conviction about communication research which we have been able to turn into a tangible enterprise during this year. I hope this book is an adequate manifesto for our shared aspirations for communication research.

My thanks to Frances Kelly for her constant support of this project. I am also grateful to Richard Stoneman of Croom Helm, who has been very patient with my mirage-like deadlines.

Finally, a special thanks to my children who have put up with my neglect. Now that this project is completed I can share their growing up without looking through them to the unfinished manuscript beyond.

If it had been possible to produce this small volume sooner, everyone concerned would have been delighted. I hope that my readers, who can probably span the book in a matter of hours, do not equate the surface clarity of this book with underlying simplicity of subject matter. There are complexities and subtleties in subject matter which have taken months to render in straightforward prose. My purpose and that of all the people who have helped me was to write a book that helped the reader to share with us a fascination for semiosis. Our collective efforts will be rewarded if a few hours reading result in a lifetime of thought and further debate.

David Sless
Canberra

WHAT IS SEMIOTICS?

And the Lord said, Behold, the people is one, and they have all
one language; and this they begin to do: and now nothing will be
restrained from them, which they have imagined to do.

(Genesis 11:6)

Introduction

Semiotics occurs whenever we stand back from our ways
of understanding and communication, and ask how these
ways of understanding and communication arise, what form they
take, and why. Semiotics is above all an intellectual curiosity
about the ways we represent our world to ourselves and each
other. It has always been a feature of human intellectual life, but
what distinguishes contemporary work in semiotics, and makes it
so exciting, is the ambition to transform this scattered and fragmented interest into a unified discipline.

Our written and spoken language, pictures, mathematics, film,
television, dress, gesture, indeed all the elements that go to make
up the communication environment which we create and in
which we are immersed, offer a rich and sometimes bewildering
variety, yet we suspect that in some basic way all these different
things have something in common. Semiotics tries to define what
it is they have in common and what distinguishes them from each
other.

We consult linguists to find out about language, art historians
or critics to find out about paintings, and anthropologists to find
out about how people in different societies signal to each other
through gesture, dress or decoration. But if we want to know
what all these different things have in common then we need to
find someone with a semiotic point of view — for semiotics is
above all else a point of view, a vantage point from which to
survey our world. It is too young to be considered a discipline,
and there are reasons why it will never become a science. But to
ask the above question of those diverse activities and to search
for an answer is to embark on a bold intellectual adventure. It

1

is a quest on a grand scale, an attempt to revoke the curse of Babel.

This book is written for the new student of semiotics and the student who has tried other sources, got lost or become confused. There is a sad irony in the fact that a subject so profoundly concerned with communication should have managed to produce so many incommunicative works. The newcomer to semiotics is often bewildered: confused by strange terminology, made uneasy by loose reasoning, concerned over an absence of method and alarmed by sweeping generalisations. Many readers, after an initial dip into these deep, muddy, turbulent waters, never venture again, either because they do not possess the stamina for swimming in such conditions, or because they assume that the stream is nothing more than effluent. While both of these reactions are understandable and to some extent justifiable, they isolate the reader from some of the most important and imaginative thought on communication and understanding in our time.

The reader already familiar with semiotic waters — their currents and movements — may find this book disorientating. The familiar terrain and well-worn channels are at times ignored and at other times visited from new directions, sometimes contrary to or against the tide of current thought. My purpose is unashamedly to redraw the map of semiotics, to provide a new perspective from which to enquire about our world.

The central argument which this book will develop is that the semiotic point of view can reach into every aspect of the world, providing a set of unifying ideas from which we can see the world afresh. At the heart of this new vision lies a single but powerful idea — semiosis. It will require the whole of this book to sketch out, even in the barest outline, the ramifications of semiosis. But in order to give the reader a glimpse of the direction in which we are ultimately heading, I shall risk a quick bold sketch of my objective.

From the muffled darkness of the womb we emerge into a noisy and ever changing visible world. We are held, looked at, talked to, and acknowledged. From the start we are enveloped in information and messages: they are a condition of existence without which there is nothing. All experience and action is mediated, transformed from one state to another, and in that transformation can be discerned the basis of semiosis, that is, the process of making and using signs. For example: a mother does not respond to the baby's hunger but to the crying which is a sign of that hunger. There is a link between the hunger and the crying, a special relation which I call the *stand-for* relation. This *stand-for* relation is ubiquitous. The circuit diagram *stands for* the electronic device, money *stands for* products and labour, flags *stand for* nations, flowers *stand for* love, and even though there seem to be wide differences in the way in which each of these things *stand for*, I shall argue that they do indeed share a common underlying process; for in these and a myriad of other circumstances is to be found our social and biological existence — societies, organisms and indeed the fabric of the universe itself are structured by a complex web of *stand-for* relations — and from a semiotic point of view the *stand-for* relation is the basis of existence.

The above paragraph is no more than a faint image of a grand picture of which this book is but a sketch. And it is by no means the first attempt to create such a picture using semiosis as a unifying principle. The ambition of semiotic inquiry in the twentieth century has been to develop a theory around this principle so that the various relations displaying this common propensity — in communication, biology or physics — can be brought together in a single explanatory framework. Like many ambitions, the visions of theoretical unity have tended to run ahead of actuality; much of what has been written is programmatic — manifestos for a grand vision. There are many different accounts of what semiotics should be and this has precipitated a far-reaching and sometimes extravagant debate about this *possible* subject; so that when someone tells us that they are an expert in semiotics, we should understand this to mean that they are knowledgeable about the debate, for there is no real subject of semiotics, no finished painting, only a tantalising possibility.

This book is an attempt to translate that possibility into actuality by searching out the simplest intellectual framework — the most economical line drawing — to sustain the idea of semiotics. Obviously such an outline will be concerned with general questions of principle but I shall address these questions through a practical problem that interests many people: how can we investigate and critically examine our vast range of forms of communication from a unified point of view? What are the common concepts, analytical tools, empirical methods, and ultimate limitations of semiotic inquiry?

The Domain of Semiotics

Every subject lays claim to a distinctive subject matter. In the case of semiotics the subject matter is vast, encompassing as it does so much of the world. There are serious and intractable problems associated with defining the boundaries of semiotics. Even the most conservatively drawn map of the area would include every aspect of our culture concerned with communication — all the arts, science and philosophy, indeed all the forms of knowledge which are passed on from one generation to the next. There are compelling arguments to suggest that the culture of communication is only the superficial landscape of semiotics, underlying which is a deep substrate which supports all forms of understanding. Such a claim could be regarded as symptomatic of a kind of intellectual imperialism or megalomania; less harshly, perhaps, it might be viewed as an attempt to create order and provide coherence in an area of confusion where differences in tradition and subject matter make cross comparisons difficult. Asking how literature, film, television, painting and other forms might be studied in a unified way is the driving curiosity behind contemporary semiotics. But, ironically, the framework that gives coherence to such diversity also takes away our delusions or hopes of imperialism; for in the search for unifying principles we shall discover finite limits to our knowledge and our control over the world. In the chapters to come I will have a great deal to say about the limits of certainty in semiotic research, and in fact one of the main contributions that semiotics can make to our intellectual life is the scepticism it can bring to critical inquiry.

The Primacy of Semiosis

In contrast to the breadth of semiotic subject matter the basic process which can be discerned in these territories has a coherence and simplicity which is much more readily accessible and identifiable. This is semiosis, the process which underlies communication and understanding, and one of the most powerful and useful concepts in the history of intellectual activity. It enables us to deal with specific issues in the study of communication and provides a way of addressing problems about the nature of existence. These more abstract questions necessarily lie ahead of us in later chapters where they will be developed fully. In this chapter we can lay the foundations by giving a simple account of semiosis.

At the outset it is necessary to understand the position that semiosis occupies within the field of semiotics. Semiotics is the study of communication and understanding, and semiosis is the process by which communication and understanding occur; it is therefore the primary process which needs to be understood in order for semiotics to develop. The study of electronics depends crucially on an understanding of the process of electron movement; without an understanding of the sub-atomic origins of electrical forces, the study of electronics is hollow. Similarly semiosis, the process on which semiotics depends, needs to be understood as a prerequisite for further inquiry. As with electronics, we would not expect the first account, offered in the opening pages of the book, to be anything more than a preliminary indication — something to point us in the right direction. None the less, we cannot escape the fact that to ask what is semiosis is to begin with the most fundamental question of this book.

The heart of semiosis is the *stand-for* relation and from a close study of its constituents we can begin to sketch in an answer to this most basic of questions. There are two readily obvious ingredients to the *stand-for* relation: an object, and whatever the object *stands for*. This is sometimes referred to in the semiotic literature as the *sign/referent* relation; the *sign stands for* something, and what it *stands for* is called its *referent*. The examples already mentioned in the introduction give a general sense of this sign/referent relation.

These two ingredients are not sufficient to describe semiosis though as we shall see some thinkers have thought the contrary. We need to ask *how* a particular sign *stands for* a particular referent, and in more general terms how it is that anything *stands for* anything. The missing ingredient is the community, individual or organism which invokes the *stand-for* relation, which uses an object (sign) to *stand for* another object (referent). This most important feature is often forgotten or taken for granted, but without the active agent, the user of signs, there would be no semiotics to study.

These three features — sign, referent and user — are minimal ingredients. The user invokes the *stand-for* relation between sign and referent, and to do so the the user must be able to distinguish between sign and referent. This is so important that it needs to be emphasised and repeated, even at the risk of pointing out the obvious. If I, as a user of signs, want to make one thing *stand for* another it is essential that I am able to distinguish between them. If the sign and the referent are indistinguishable, then it is meaningless even to talk about one standing for the other, for they are the same. The *stand-for* relation can only be invoked between things which are taken to be different from each other by the user.

Beginning Semiotic Research

When embarking on a new subject of study it is appropriate to ask what is the object being studied and what are the smallest units out of which the subject is built. As we have seen, we constantly return to the *stand-for* relation. It is the heart of the semiotic universe and its basic building block. In Chapter 12, when many other arguments are in place, I shall demonstrate a peculiar characteristic of semiosis, namely its irreducibility; it is impossible to separate the components of the *stand-for* relation of semiosis from each other; within the semiotic point of view there cannot be anything simpler or more basic than the triad of semiosis formed between sign, referent and user. At this stage I can hint at the nature of this remarkable feature of semiosis by using an analogy.

Semiosis can be thought of as being like a polygon: if the sides are taken apart and placed alongside each other then it is no longer possible to talk about the figure, even though all the pieces are there; the pieces do not of themselves make up the original shape, only their organisation into a particular pattern. In the case of both the geometric form and semiosis, the pattern is an essential part of the definition of what they are. Semiosis differs from a geometric form in that its pattern is not spatial but abstract; it is a pattern of three interrelated ideas arranged in a triad through the operation of the *stand-for* relation.

The irreducibility of semiosis provides the first principle of semiotic research:

In semiotic research, statements about users, signs or referents can never be made in isolation from each other. A statement about one always contains implications about the other two.

The best way to demonstrate this principle is through an example. (At this early stage of presenting ideas about semiotic research, any example must be highly simplified; we cannot address the full complexity of the subject without careful preparation and this opening example will prepare the way for fuller treatments of the subject in later chapters.)

In Figure 1.1 is a public information symbol. Notice that even the name 'public information symbol' contains implications about the three parts of semiosis. In a vague way it tells us who the user is:

Figure 1.1: Airport Symbol

the public. Even without a replica of the symbol in front of us many of us could probably imagine from the name what sort of sign it might be and also the kind of thing to which it might refer. Once these statements are made with greater specificity it is possible to get a clearer sense of their importance and interdependence. Firstly turning our attention to the sign it is important to realise that what we are looking at above is itself a sign of a sign; it *stands for* the many versions of this sign which are to be found in public places. This could make our discussion quite complex since we are discussing the sign at one remove. I shall return to this important problem in Chapter 7 where we can deal with its implications in more detail. For the moment I shall assume that we are talking about the sign in its public location. Next we turn our attention to its referent and it is here, when we give an account of what it refers to, that we begin to see the importance of the interdependence of the three statements. If people are asked what they think this sign refers to they do not always give the same answer. Three answers which have been given are 'airport', 'low-flying aircraft' or simply 'aircraft' (Sless and Cairney 1982b). Each of these answers involves the three components of semiosis and there are differences which arise in each. Each of the referents is given by a different user and even though superficially the sign in each instance seems to be the same, it may not necessarily be so. When a person gives the response 'low-flying aircraft', does it mean that the sign looks to him as though it is a picture of an aircraft close to the ground? We could not attempt to answer that question without a great deal more information but asking it raises the possibility that two people looking at the same physical object may not necessarily see it in quite the same way. If we acknowledge this possibility we must be prepared to accept that even the most independent part of the semiotic triad, the sign, is potentially changeable as a consequence of changes in the other components.

It is therefore not possible to make statements about the sign's referent in the abstract; there is always an implication that there is a user for whom it has that referent. The dangers of not following this principle are many but the most persistent arises from the false assumption that the sign has an independent existence from the other parts. One way in which this assumption is often disguised is by implicitly assuming that the authority which controls the use of the sign controls the referent. So a statement about the referent of a sign, if we unpack it, is more accurately a statement about what the sign is officially used to designate. As we shall see in later chapters, questions of authority are never far away in semiotics. But even if we accept that for certain purposes the 'official' referent of this symbol may be important it is not necessarily more important for all purposes. Psychologists or anthropologists might be much more interested in the range of referents used than in the one official referent; they may be interested in demonstrating how people display diversity and challenge authority by inventing their own referents for signs. These researchers, guided by their own interests, are *users* of the sign; for them it *stands for* a great deal more than the 'official' referent. By contrast a designer employed to improve the quality of the symbol's performance would want to restrict the range of different referents that might be applied by people and this would make the designer a very different kind of user of the sign. Thus we can see how the statements about the sign and its referent are inextricably linked to the users. It is also possible to see how we might ordinarily gloss over these interdependent statements or conflate them, reducing this network of interdependence to a single proposition — 'this sign *stands for* x'. There are many moments in the history of semiotic research where the above principle has been neglected and we shall have occasion to examine some of its consequences.

Conclusions

Something of the peculiar nature of semiotics should begin to make itself felt with this first principle. Unlike many fields of inquiry, semiotics is not primarily concerned with facts or the organising of those facts into known categories. Semiotics is much more obviously concerned with relations; how, when we make one kind of statement, others are entailed. Many unresolved issues surround the application of the first principle of semiotic research elaborated above and therefore it must be thought of as a first approximation that will be progressively refined as the arguments in this book unfold.

Summary

Semiotics is the study of all manifestations of the *stand-for* relation. It is an attempt to apply a single explanatory framework to a wide variety of phenomena. In particular it has been applied to many aspects of culture including the arts, sciences and philosophy. At the heart of semiotics is semiosis — the process of making and using signs. Semiosis comprises signs, referents and users in an indissoluble triad. This triad provides the foundation for semiotic research.

2 COMMUNICATION

Ships that pass in the night, and speak each other in passing;
Only a signal shown and a distant voice in the darkness;
So on the ocean of life we pass and speak one another,
Only a look and a voice; then darkness again and a silence.

(Longfellow)

Introduction

Many people (including myself) come to semiotics because of an interest in communication. Semiotics is concerned with signs in general, and as signs are the stuff out of which messages are made it seems almost inevitable that an interest in communication will lead to semiotics. Like many newcomers I found semiotic texts peculiarly opaque, but when I had clarified what they had to say about communication, I was surprised and disappointed to discover how little the subject advanced my understanding. I assumed, like many students in a new area, that authoritative voices had long since pronounced on my naive and unsophisticated doubts and questions — illuminating the dark spaces with the light of wisdom. The tone of much writing in semiotics is nothing if not authoritative; at times the style is even imperial, seeking to embrace the whole of humanity within its domain. As a mere subject of the empire I took my initial inability to understand what was said as a symptom of my own intellectual inferiority, but as I probed further I began to realise that the emperor was, to say the least, very thinly clad.

The doubts and questions which had aroused my initial curiosity were still unresolved, so I began to search for my own solutions. This chapter is an account of my search for a deeper understanding of communication, without which I could not make progress in my search for understanding in semiotics. It builds on some of the ideas I developed in an earlier book, *Learning and Visual Communication* (Sless 1981). To the reader, impatient for a progression of ideas in semiotics, this exploration of communication may seem like a diversion. It is not. We cannot progress in semiotics without a clear sense of the problematic nature of communication.

Raymond Williams in *Keywords* (Williams 1976) provides a suc-
cinct summary of the history and origins of the two senses of communication which are to be found at work in contemporary
debates. Communication first appeared in its modern usage in the
fifteenth century as an action 'to make common to many'. By the
end of the fifteenth century 'communication' had become a noun
— the 'object thus made common'. However, from the late seven-
teenth century a new sense emerged which extended its use to cover
the *means* of communication. In this more modern sense it was
often used as a generalised way of referring to transport systems,
particularly during the main period of development of roads,
canals and railways. In the twentieth century it has come to refer
more to the means of conveying information and ideas rather
than goods and people; *transmission* has been emphasised in this
usage. These etymological differences are important, as Raymond
Williams suggests:

In controversy about communication systems and communication theory it is often useful to recall the unresolved range of the
original noun of action, represented at its extremes by *transmit*, a
one-way process, and *share* (cf. *communion* and especially *com-
municant*), a common or mutual process. The intermediate
senses — make common to many, and impart — can be read in
either direction, and the choice is often crucial. (Williams 1976,
p. 63)

As is often the case, I came to understand Williams's insight
after I had struggled with these problems on my own. Williams
clarifies the agenda of the contemporary debate in this area as he
does in so many other areas related to the study of communication
in society. But my own reflections did not lead me to take up either
of these positions. Rather, I began to realise that there was something wrong with both and that to advance our understanding in
semiotics we need a new and more radical sense of communication.
Williams gives us an agenda for a debate that has already taken
place and which has failed to come to a resolution. I would like to
start a new argument.

I shall begin with a close look at the idea of communication as
transmission and then progress to the idea of *sharing*. In both I will
point to problems that cannot be resolved. This will set the scene
for something new.

Communication as Transmission

I began my interest in communication in the 1960s as an under-
graduate in psychology and sociology, two disciplines greatly preoccupied with their scientific status — though there was generally
more talk about science than evidence of scientific success, particularly in the American work which dominated at that time. It
was clear that the natural sciences and their highly successful technological offspring were taken as models for these younger
subjects. Even when the theories and findings of these admirers of
so-called hard science were vague and inconclusive there was a
tendency to present the subject using terminology and concepts that
had the appearance of science and precision. The emerging studies
of the psychology and sociology of communication were no exception and the favoured model used to account for human communication was taken from electronic communication engineering.

It seemed that a generalised model derived from the electronic
marvel of radio *transmission* was an ideal metaphor for the richly
complex and confusing variety of human communication. Right
from the start the researchers in this field could take comfort in the
scientific status of their study, by referring to the impeccable
credentials of their technological model, and so a formal account
of electronic systems quickly became adapted to systems of human
communication.

The unwieldy field of human communication could be reduced
to a series of manageable areas each of which could be isolated as a
component and studied separately or in relation to the other components. The diagrams in Figure 2.2 need to be examined closely in
order to see the common pattern which they share. Even though
they are taken from texts studying different kinds of human communication, they break up the process into three domains: all the
activities or processes which go towards the making of messages,
the domain of the message itself, and the domain of the receiver of
the message. These three seemingly independent ingredients of the
communication process become apparent in Figure 2.3 where the
general pattern has been superimposed over each of the Figure 2.2
diagrams.

This is a compelling view of communication; it seems natural and
uncontentious. It is hard to realise that this all too solid account of
communication is in fact a metaphor — human communication is
being treated *as if* it were like an electronic transmission network.

Figure 2.1

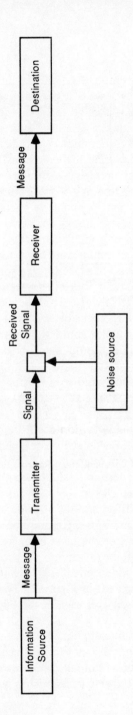

Source: After Shannon and Weaver 1949

Figure 2.2

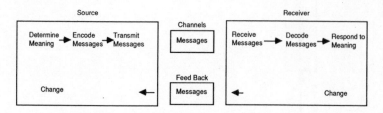

After McCrosky and Wheeles, Introduction to Human Communication, (Allyn and Bacon Inc., Boston 1976)

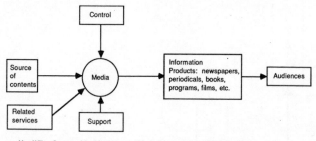

After Wilber Scramm, Men Messages and Media (Harper & Row, New York, 1973)

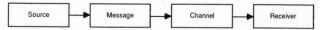

(After David Berlo, The Process of Communication (Rinehart Press, San Fransisco, 1960)

Source: After David Berlo, The Process of Communication (Rinehart Press, San Francisco, 1960)

Figure 2.3

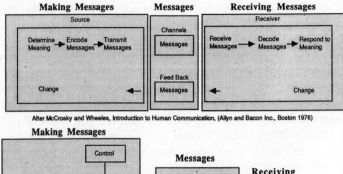

After McCrosky and Wheeles, Introduction to Human Communication, (Allyn and Bacon Inc., Boston 1976)

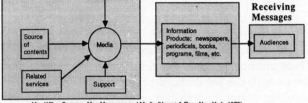

After Wilber Scramm, Men Messages and Media (Harper & Row, New York, 1973)

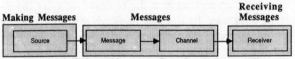

(After David Berlo, The Process of Communication (Rinehart Press, San Fransisco, 1960)

Source: After David Berlo, The Process of Communication (Rinehart Press, San Francisco, 1960)

There have been many occasions in the history of science when a mechanical metaphor has served as a basis for an advance in knowledge, for example Harvey's use of the pump as a metaphor for the workings of the heart in the circulatory system. The success of such metaphors has encouraged researchers to use them and the tangible quality of the objects from which they derive lends them a vicarious validity so that they seem beyond doubt. The electronic metaphor of human communication is undoubtedly powerful, because many researchers still cling to it as the solid framework in which their findings should be presented, even though, as I will show, it has had a history of failed applications and disappointing findings.

If we return to its most generalised form in the mathematical theory of communication (Figure 2.1) we can begin to unravel the reasons why the faith in this idea was mistaken. Let us take a radio receiver and transmitter as typical examples of the electronic devices which fit this model and compare them with speaking and listening. There are obvious material similarities; the radio transmitter corresponds to the vocal chords; the radio waves generated by the transmitter correspond to the airwaves generated by the vocal chords; and the receiver corresponds to the ear. The idea that a transmitter encodes information and the receiver decodes information seems to be paralleled by the way in which the vocal chords encode words into airwaves and the ears decode this physical energy back into words. These similarities are the basis for retention of the metaphor but they hide a deep difference.

Given two radio receivers, an electronics engineer could form a comparative judgement about their performance by measuring in a laboratory the inputs, outputs, waveform characteristics and so on of the two devices, and the results could be checked independently by an engineer in a different laboratory.

Now let us imagine a comparable study of human listeners. Can we, using a similar method of study, arrive at a comparative judgement of their performance? We could certainly wire them up to all kinds of measuring equipment and determine their physiological reactions. Clearly such a study is technically possible, but with the exception of abnormalities at the physical level, it would not tell us which of the two was the better listener.

To study human communication we need something that differs from the engineer's measuring instruments. At the very least, whoever conducted the study would have to be competent in language. This requirement may seem simple and straightforward but it involves a radical distension of the metaphor, because we are now no longer exclusively concerned with the objects studied or the instruments used; we are now interested in factors outside the technical model, namely, the researcher's performance. Perhaps the method of research used might be to engage the listener in conversation. The role of the researcher in this method is significantly different to that of the electronics engineer in two ways. Firstly the researcher acts as a transmitter and a receiver *within* the network, and secondly, the researcher judges the receiver's performance on the basis of his own understanding of the language. This would be equivalent to our electronic engineer becoming a radio transmitter, then judging the performance of a receiver by becoming a radio receiver himself and finally, as if the transformation from engineer to radio were not difficult enough, he would have to compare his own performance against the radios under study! Clearly what seems to us perfectly reasonable in the study of human communication becomes utterly ridiculous when we try to apply the same logic to the study of electronic systems. And when we apply the methods of the electronic engineer to human communication we seem to miss what is most interesting.

From the point of view of the electronics engineer the diagram in Figure 2.1 represents his field of study and he, the engineer, is *outside* the diagram looking in. We can see how this way of describing the relationship of the engineer to the diagram perfectly reflects the ideal relationship between a scientist and what he studies. As far as possible the scientist must be detached from the object of study — a neutral observer who does not influence the material being studied. As we have seen, the study of human communication requires the researcher to become involved in the subject matter under investigation in a way which is quite different. Far from being on the outside of the diagram looking in, the researcher is actually *in the diagram*.

Communication as Sharing

European semiotics originating with the French linguist Saussure tries to deal with the problem of the researcher's involvement obliquely by addressing a different kind of question: what is the nature of the language which we *share*? If each member of a particular culture shares with others a common language then, in principle, any member of the culture can study the object they have in common. From this point of view the problem of whether one is outside or inside simply disappears; everyone *shares* the same language, therefore we are all inside. The European tradition of semiotic research has been dominated by this idea of communication as sharing:

> Language exists in the form of a sum of impressions deposited in the brain of each member of a community, almost like a dictionary of which identical copies have been distributed to each individual. Language exists in each individual, yet it is common to all. (Saussure 1974, p. 19)

Following the lead of Saussure, many European researchers have assumed, without further questioning, that everyone within a particular culture shares the same understanding of language. Any individual member of a culture has access to the same vocabulary and grammar and hence, in principle, can study the structure of that language and its rules. The main question is then one of defining the nature of the shared understanding.

Some researchers have taken Saussure's ideas about language and applied them to other means of conveying meaning — such as film, television, advertising or fashion — assuming that these too are similarly shared and hence accessible for study to any member of a particular culture. Because Saussure has been a major formative influence on certain kinds of semiotic research of which I am highly critical, and against which I have reacted, I have devoted part of Chapter 11 to a more detailed study of his ideas and the way they have been used. In this chapter I only want to look at the viability of the central idea of communication as sharing which Saussure uses in his work and which is used by many other students who followed him.

In order to give a substantial quality to this presumed shared basis of understanding it has become common among researchers following Saussure to use the term *system* to refer to the collective nature of language. This is misleading for many reasons which will become apparent as the arguments in this book unfold. In its place I shall use the idea of an *infrastructure of understanding*.

One of the commonest ways of thinking about communication, as I showed earlier in this chapter, is in terms of hardware; the machinery which is used for transmitting and receiving messages is taken to be a model of the entire process, and in our time this usually means electronic technology. The policy of most governments and the attention of their critics have been directed towards the control, ownership and presumed power of the technological infrastructure which is made up of such things as satellites, broadcasting systems and newspaper production. But there is a less obvious though equally important resource and that is the capacity of a society to generate and sustain ways of understanding; without the second, the first is useless. Putting the matter very simply, there is little point in having hardware systems that can deliver megabytes of information that nobody can understand or make use of. When the hardware is in place and every home or workplace is wired we will not suddenly emerge into the communication equivalent of the Garden of Eden; it is much more likely that we will create a new Tower of Babel, unless we pay attention to the languages we use and the capacity of people to understand them. Thus the infrastructure of understanding must be considered alongside the technological infrastructure.

The Fragile Infrastructure

It is not generally realised how fragile and vulnerable is the infrastructure of understanding. Following Saussure and others who have emphasised the shared aspect of languages there has been a tendency to gloss over the breaks, fissures and chasms which characterise this infrastructure in favour of holistic approaches which seem to examine the nature of such constructs as 'linguistic competence', the 'logic of culture' or 'discursive practices' — in short *The System*. But the indications of fragility are there to see and, tempting though the idea of shared understanding might be, it is as well to begin from the premise that communication is based not on the clear evidence of shared understanding but on the *belief* of shared understanding.

Consider our written language. No other form of communication is quite so intensively and uniformly taught in our systems of education. If we were to seek a standard against which to judge attainable *shared* competence in different forms of communication we would expect, given the social effort we expend and the importance we attach to the achievement of literacy, that the general competence in reading and writing would offer us a target to aim for.

The experience of those battling at the front line of communication with the public at large is not encouraging. The recent British government report *Forms Under Control* which was highly critical of civil service forms for public use had this to say about the public's competence in this most intensively cultivated area:

> . . . about one in 20 of the adult population have a reading age of less than nine. In all, about one quarter of Britain's adults fail to reach a reading age of 13 as measured by UNESCO literacy standards. (Central Management Library 1982)

Measures of literacy are notoriously crude but they reveal in a general way that the capacity of people to make use of this resource is not uniform *despite* the massive expenditure of public funds to develop shared competence in this part of the infrastructure.

When we turn to other parts of the infrastructure the evidence is even more disconcerting. Television is regarded by many as a powerful component of this infrastructure because it is believed to be easily and widely understood, but this may not be so. In the USA a large representative sample survey of the population revealed that:

> The vast majority of television viewers — more than 90 percent — misunderstand some part of what they see, no matter what kind of broadcast they are watching. Normally the range of misunderstanding is between one-fourth and one-third of any broadcast, whether it is an entertainment–news program, commercial or public service announcement. Regardless of what they are watching, television viewers seem to misunderstand facts as much as they misunderstand inferences in a broadcast. (AAAA Educational Foundation 1980, p. 1)

This finding is consistent with other research conducted in Finland which revealed that, even with the help of the interviewer, 48 per cent of people questioned immediately after watching the news could recall nothing of the content (Nordenstreng 1971). And this finding has been replicated with Australian viewers (Powell *et al.* 1980).

Part of the myth of television potency is based on the belief that visual forms of communication are somehow more easily understood than others. If we look at public information symbols, one of the most widespread forms of visual communication, which is even thought to be a *lingua franca* in the form of international symbols, the evidence is even more alarming. In a recent international study (Easterby and Graydon 1981) of an extensive range of different symbols, some of which are widely used, only three symbols were clearly understood by more than two-thirds of the respondents and two of these were not pictorial symbols but conventional — a cross for hospital and a *P* for parking. Of the 108 symbols tested 86 were understood clearly by less than 50 per cent of the sample, yet 32 of the symbols in this group are in wide use. These kinds of figures are not unusual and have been turning up repeatedly in international and national studies over the last 20 years (Mackie 1967; Easterby and Zwaga 1976; Easterby and Hakiel 1977; Sless and Cairney 1980, 1982a,b; Cairney, Campbell and Sless 1981).

The infrastructure of understanding is therefore unlike its technological counterpart; and it is readily obvious that more efficient forms of information *transmission* are not necessarily going to lead to better communication or *sharing* but to more, though undoubtedly faster, misunderstandings.

The Two Faces of the Infrastructure

There are further characteristics of this infrastructure that distinguish it from its technical counterpart. It has two faces: on the one hand there is the conglomerate of loosely defined and vaguely applied conventions which are sometimes mistakenly referred to as codes (O'Sullivan *et al.* 1983), and on the other hand there is the distribution and nature of competence in these conventions within the population. Taking language as an example: on the one hand there is the loose system of rules known as grammar, and on the other hand there are the many colloquial, idiomatic and individual variations in language use. These are not separable, as my analysis might suggest; they are merely the two sides of the same coin. The only way we can even begin describing the conventions is from a position of competence, so that the researcher faces from the outset the problem of his or her own *position within* the field of inquiry. The communication researcher cannot therefore take refuge in the idea of communication as sharing as a way of avoiding the problem of position. As I have shown earlier in this chapter, there is no

outsider's position, no place of scholarly detachment or objec
tivity; but equally it is impossible to submerge oneself into th
presumed shared homogeneity of the group.

As a consequence of the involvement of the researcher, ther
arises a curious problem: when reading communication researc}
how do we judge the competence of the researcher? If, fo
example, someone conducts an analysis of television content, hov
can we be certain that he is competent in the necessary convention
for understanding television? Taking at face value the USA
research I mentioned earlier, there is a high probability that th
researcher will come from those in the population (over 90 per cent
who misunderstand between one-quarter and one-third of wha
they see!

A great deal of the communication research has taken fo1
granted the competence of the researcher and has assumed tha
competence within the population is either homogeneous, or clearl}
specifiable within simplistic demographic, cultural, or economi<
categories.

In many studies, the loose conventions of which I spoke ar<
treated by communication researchers as objects of study with a1
independent existence — there to be excavated from the interstice:
of messages. This curious ontology has created a generation o1
solipsistic scholars who, by assuming that their own competence i:
adequately representative of everybody else's, are actually studyin{
themselves and their own readings of texts, offering their imagination as evidence.

Communication in an Age of Doubt

The arguments presented above are the result of applying a
rigorous scepticism to the concept of communication. Communication, as defined above, is the result of an erosion of certainty and
a sedimentation of doubt. Another way in which we can come to
this conclusion is by setting the idea of communication within an
historical context and looking at its changing meaning.

Communication as sharing arose from a period in social history
when societies were smaller, less subject to change, and inward-
looking. Communication as transmission developed in a period of
rapid social expansion when large empires were formed spanning
the globe. As sea, rail, road and air links spread like tentacles to

encompass the globe so the culture of those who controlled this network followed. For those in power, it was easier to assume that the battle over hearts and minds could be won by analogous means to the battle for the market place; transport systems carried goods and money, communication systems would carry information and ways of understanding which served the economic interests. We are now at a point in this process when the communication systems cover the globe like a mesh. We are closer than we have ever been to the possibility of universal understanding — McLuhan's vision of the 'Global Village' (McLuhan 1964) — and yet ironically the very instruments expected to impose this accord provide daily accounts of conflict, disagreement and misunderstanding. For example, at a time when the mass media stereotyping of women was at its most sexist and pervasive there emerged a powerful feminist lobby to counter this view. The same may be said of anti-nuclear, consumer and environmental lobbies. If communication functioned by transmission to homogenise the public mind, none of these movements should exist. Nor should we be assailed on all sides by doubts about our political and social values. We even doubt our own survival as a species. In such a climate it is not surprising that our certainties and assurance about the concepts we use should also be swept aside in favour of a more uncertain, less confident manner.

Communication as sharing looks backward to a romantic notion of community that we can never recapture, even assuming that it ever existed; the curse of Babel has probably always been there, waiting in the wings to overwhelm us at any moment with confusion and misunderstanding. Transmission as a concept of communication is firmly rooted in the ideology of imperialism. Once we question the authority of the imperialist we must also question the validity of his intellectual postures.

Summary

Communication has two conflicting senses: 'transmission' and 'sharing'. The idea of communication as transmission cannot be successfully applies to human communication research, because, unlike the engineer studying electronic networks, the researcher into human communication cannot be a detached observer. The idea of sharing also presents problems because there is considerable doubt about the extent to which competence in languages is shared.

3 COMMUNICATION AND POSITION

> . . . if you stick a Babel fish in your ear you can instantly understand anything said to you in any form of language. . . . the poor Babel fish, by effectively removing all barriers to communication between different races and cultures, has caused more and bloodier wars than anything else in the history of creation.
>
> (Douglas Adams 1979)

Introduction

In the last chapter I showed how the two major concepts of communication which have guided research lead to problems: communication viewed as a process of *transmission* follows the scientific convention of excluding the researcher from the object of study whereas in fact the researcher is always inside and part of what is studied; communication viewed as *sharing* acknowledges the researcher as an insider but fails to recognise that being an insider does not automatically mean that one shares the same understanding as everyone else.

There has been a long and sterile debate in communication research about the relationship between researchers and the messages, texts or discourses of study. The debate has focused on questions of objectivity or subjectivity, as if a simple dichotomy between two *positions* were sufficient to deal with the complexity of relations within communication. In this chapter I shall argue that we need to move beyond simple notions of *position* such as insiders or outsiders, subjective or objective, and articulate a comprehensive *logic of positions*. Additionally, I shall lay down the foundations of the *logic* which will then be developed more fully in later chapters. This requires some radical re-thinking of ideas about communication. Initially this entails a closer look at why the idea of communication as sharing is, despite its weakness, important. Secondly, objectivity and subjectivity need to be seen in a new light. This will provide the necessary groundwork for the major part of this chapter which will explore a new way of thinking about communication.

24

Abandoning Sharing

It will seem to many that abandoning the idea of sharing is too radical a step. I will however, demonstrate that sharing, as such, is not a necessary ingredient of communication but a *belief* in sharing is essential. The best way to get a sense of this idea is to look at situations in which we are on the boundary between what is and what is not communication. In *Learning and Visual Communication* (1981) I gave the following example:

> In 1968 a group of radio astronomers discovered, almost by accident, the existence of a radio source which showed regular fluctuations in energy. Nothing like it had ever been discovered before and there was a flurry of excitement and speculation about its origins and causes.
>
> As the days went by the excitement rose when we found that the pulses were coming from a body no larger than a planet situated relatively close to us among the nearer stars of our galaxy. Were the pulses some kind of message from another civilization? This possibility was entertained only for lack of an obvious natural explanation for signals that seemed so artificial. (Hewish 1968)
>
> Here is the knife edge of the distinction between what is and what is not communication; on one side a natural phenomenon without acceptable explanation and on the other a message with an unknown author.

There is no actual sharing, only the excitement of possible sharing. What distinguishes the pulse as message from the pulse as natural phenomenon is the presence of an imagined author on whom the hope of sharing can be projected.

The absence of actual sharing can be clearly seen in another example which straddles the boundary between what is and what is not communication. Many events in the Bible — the rainbow after the flood, the burning bush, the parting of the Red Sea are examples — can be viewed in two distinct ways. Hard-headed scientific explanation has it that, even supposing them to have actually occurred, these events are explicable as natural happenings due entirely to the operation of the laws of nature. By contrast a religious explanation accepts them as indications of the existence of

God and as specific acts from that source. These different descriptions draw on different world views. There can be no doubt that there are people who believe in miracles and for them these events are messages. From their point of view miracles are a form of communication between God and themselves. God's existence as a communicator is not a matter of fact; it is importantly a matter of construction, imagination. God is believed to exist through an act of imagination. What does exist is a relationship between a receiver and a supposed message. In other words, from a receiver's *position*, what is minimally necessary is the construction of an author — a sender of the message. The sharing — the sense of communion — arises as a logical consequence of the construction of the sender. The constructed sender is logically prior to the *hope* of sharing.

In these borderline cases, sharing with another entity — whether it be god or alien — does not have to occur in fact, even though the hope and belief in sharing is clearly present. But even without any actual sharing, both are, in principle, acts of communication. It could be argued that these are instances of unsuccessful communication and that communication proper involves a sharing of understanding. Unfortunately, the evidence of empirical research does not support this proposition. The research I quoted in the last chapter is only a fragment of a much larger body of evidence examining many different kinds of communication. In fact, if there is any single empirical generalisation which has emerged from communications research within the last twenty years to which most empirical researchers would assent, it is that shared understanding between sender and receiver can never be taken for granted.

Communication, Semiotics and Lying

All the examples I have given so far involve communication at a distance and it may seem to some readers that intimate social relations involving conversation are relatively free of these problems and in that context it is still legitimate to refer to communication as a process of sharing. The presumed intimacy of conversation has led some to think that speech is in some sense a privileged form of communication, providing the participants with a direct access to each other's thoughts; the link between receiver and sender would be, as it were, transparent, and the message would merely be the vehicle through which their thoughts would pass. However, a moment's reflection will reveal that even among people who know each other very well, the rule of intimacy is by no means assured and may indeed be the exception.

There can be very few people who do not know what it means to lie. Indeed it might well be the case that lying is central to communication and hence semiotics. Umberto Eco, a leading Italian semiotician, very perceptively suggested that

> [S]*semiotics is in principle the discipline studying everything which can be used in order to lie.* (Eco 1976b, p. 7)

Sissela Bok, who has written one of the few books dealing with lying, offers a definition of deception and lying that quite clearly locates them *within* communication and reinforces Eco's insight:

> When we undertake to deceive others intentionally, we communicate messages meant to mislead them, meant to make them believe what we ourselves do not believe. We can do so through gesture, through disguise, by means of inaction, even through silence. . . . I shall define as a lie any intentionally deceptive message which is *stated*. Such statements are most often made verbally or in writing, but can of course also be conveyed via smoke signals, Morse code, sign language and the like. (Bok 1978, p. 13)

I have already cast some doubt on whether we do in fact uniformly share the same languages. Bok points out that even if we do share the same languages we might not use them in order to share experience. But there can be no doubt that lying is *part of* communication, not something apart or even necessarily aberrant.

Julian Jaynes in his bold speculation on the origins of consciousness suggests the possibility that lying may have been necessary in order to survive during periods of social upheaval, and may have precipitated the emergence of consciousness:

> Long term deceit requires the invention of an analog self that can 'do' or 'be' something quite different from what a person actually does or is, as seen by his associates. It is an easy matter to imagine how important for survival during the centuries such

an ability would be. Overrun by invaders . . . if a man could be one thing on the inside and another thing on the outside, could harbor his hatred and revenge behind a mask of acceptance of the inevitable, such a man would survive. Or . . . being commanded by invading strangers, perhaps in a strange language, the person who could obey superficially and have 'within him' another self with 'thoughts' contrary to his disloyal actions, who could loathe the man he smiled at, would be much more successful in perpetuating himself and his family in the new millennium. (Jaynes 1982, pp. 219–20)

One very simple consequence of a lie is that it involves *not sharing* one's thoughts with someone else. The central point to understand about semiotic phenomena is that they involve the *stand-for* relation which operates quite differently from other kinds of relations. For example if we talk about causal relations we think of one event always preceding another: ice melts because of a rise in temperature, so that when we see the ice melt we take that to be a *reliable* indication that it is getting warmer. In other words we do not expect the melting of ice to tell us a lie about the temperature. Indeed so sure are we of some kinds of relations, which we call causal, that it seems preposterous to even think about the possibility of lies in this area. But if someone came in out of the cold and said 'it is getting warmer' or 'the ice is melting' we might believe them but we could never rule out the possibility that they were lying; and it is that possibility which points to one of the distinctive characteristics of the *stand-for* relation.

As many people discover from bitter experience, our conversations, which can seem the greatest source of intimacy and understanding, can on occasions be the source of deception and failure to comprehend. Any adequate theory of communication must deal with lies as well as truth. It is a curious fact of Western scholarship that there are endless treatises on the subject of truth but few on lying (see Bok (1978) and Goffman (1974) for important exceptions). It is as if the weight of the former were intended to crush the other out of existence. Yet our private and public lives are filled with both. Lying is the repressed taboo of our intellectual life, just as sex is sometimes the repressed taboo of social life. The liar paradox of traditional philosophy would have been far more intriguing and would have led to many more interesting insights if instead of the form it normally takes, 'All Cretans are liars', it had taken the form 'All Cretans *can* lie'.

Neither conversation nor speech, therefore, has a specially privi-leged position among forms of communication as custodian mes-sengers of thoughts. We can claim that they are the most frequently used, the best developed or the most flexible, but these attributes are equally at the disposal of truth or lies, and if one can tell a great truth through speech then one can also tell a grand lie. Perhaps because of its ubiquity and power, we take conversation between two people who know each other to be the model of all other forms of communication and our idealised expectations of intimate relations are transferred to all forms of communication. Thus it is not surprising that critics have on occasions argued that a painting, or a novel, or a film can provide access to the thoughts and feelings of their producers. But as with conversation, all these forms can deceive as much as they can illuminate; they can shed both light and dark.

The main point I wish to make is that sharing, which is often assumed to be a *necessary* and defining characteristic of communi-cation, may not be so. There is no set of universally agreed con-ditions that can ensure that the relation between sender and receiver in communication will involve sharing. If the sharing of under-standing were a defining characteristic of normal communication, then there would be a great deal of what we would ordinarily call communication which would fall short of this standard of normality.

I would not expect many readers to relinquish their faith in com-munication as a sharing process but I would like at the very least to set that faith in a sceptical framework. In other words *we should not take for granted the idea that communication involves sharing; rather we should always ask, in any instance, whether sharing is actually taking place.* But we are still left with the strong conviction that sharing is important to our understanding of communication. Despite the evidence or arguments we still want to retain the idea of sharing. For even if communication is not always a process of sharing we might want it to be so.

The idea of sharing is importantly an aspect of our ideology; one of our deeply held beliefs about the nature of the society we live in. As I shall demonstrate repeatedly in this book, belief in sharing recurs at crucial moments in debates about how communication works in society. The idea of sharing is crucial to the notion of society but it may be that social cohesion is more powerfully affected by a widespread *belief* in sharing than by evidence of its presence. We believe in sharing because without it the very fabric of social life is threatened. *When we define communication as a process of sharing we are not describing how things are but how we would like them to be.* It is for this reason that the notion of communication as sharing remains of value to us despite the arguments and evidence.

Objectivity and Subjectivity

Semiotics studies messages and in order to study messages we have to read them. A reader is always a participant, never an observer, and to participate involves being in a *position* on the *inside* not an observer on the outside. Unfortunately the normal way in which scholars have dealt with the problem of their own position is by invoking ideas of scholarly objectivity. To be objective is to be neutral, disinterested, detached from the material one is investigating — so that one can approach one's subject matter without influencing or affecting it. Objectivity is the first rung on the ladder to omniscience. It is no coincidence that science is seen by some as having usurped the role of religion. The spirituality of the priest with its implied nearness to deity and omnipotence has been replaced by the objectivity of the scientist and its nearness to omniscience.

To be subjective, by contrast, is to acknowledge one's own interest, and be part of the world, inextricably woven into the pattern of things — unreflecting and guided by feeling. Traditionally we are inclined to see rationality as the province of objectivity and feelings as the province of subjectivity.

Philosophers of science have demonstrated that true objectivity is unattainable — an ideal. In practice all attempts at objectivity are inevitably tainted with subjectivity. It is as if science — the usurper to the throne of religion — has discovered that it too is tainted with original sin; no scientist can escape the blemish of subjectivity. Objectivity is unattainable yet desirable as subjectivity is inevitable yet reprehensible. We are, it seems, caught between heaven and hell. Yet this impasse does not seem to affect the despotic style of intellectual rhetoric.

Objectivity may be unattainable, omniscience a mere chimera, but many of our forms of discourse are prefigured in omniscience;

the author can occupy, as a matter of social convention, a god-like position.

We have a variety of styles of discourse which allow and encourage authors to believe that they can disengage from the text, that they can speak as if from outside or beyond its subject matter: the omniscient narrator in fiction, the judge sifting evidence, the scientist or scholar studying data and arguments, the reporter describing events. These modes of discourse are so commonly used — so much part of our commonsense understanding — that even when the necessary intellectual arguments exist for a sceptical challenge these modes persist; they do so partly because we accept without question the imperialism on which they are founded. We accept as normal the right to exert authority and power over the subjects we investigate — imposing our will but remaining detached.

As will be apparent from the arguments so far developed, such a vantage point may at the very least be questionable in the study of communication. The alternative, however, is not the pit of subjectivity but an articulation of the variety of positions it is possible to occupy within the process of communication.

Communication as Position

My search for an understanding of communication has led me to consider different kinds of metaphors. I do not think that there is a single metaphor that will encompass all the subtleties of the process but at this stage in the development of my argument there is a great deal to recommend a metaphor based on the idea of a landscape within which are located both the researcher and the object of study. How the landscape appears to the researcher depends very much on the position from which he views it; as the position he occupies changes so does the scene, and as certain views become visible, others disappear.

I shall replace the engineer's diagram of the last chapter with a diagram in which we can locate ourselves (Figure 3.1). It might be difficult to imagine this peculiar relationship towards a diagram; our cultural habits of looking at diagrams are so frequently scientific and detached. But there are some interesting exceptions. The most notable are maps, when we use them to find our way. This kind of diagram can be a great comfort and source of information

Figure 3.1: Diagram of London Underground System

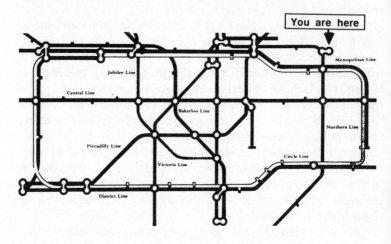

to the intrepid traveller lost in the intestinal labyrinth of London's underground and its usefulness stems from the fact that it is possible to locate oneself *inside the diagram*. From this 'perspective' it is possible to see one of the major weaknesses in all the diagrams in Chapter 2: they have all excluded the researcher. They pretend that the student of communication is outside, like the engineer. This makes the subject seem scientific but it has, as will now be apparent, caused many researchers to lose their way. But before abandoning the engineer's diagram completely I will use it to get our bearings and commence preliminary survey work. For our purposes we need a simple generalised version of the diagram and we can derive this from Figure 2.3.

Figure 3.2

My choice of vocabulary to describe the basic ingredients of all communication processes follows a widespread practice among other recent researchers, so Figure 3.2 should not be thought of as applying exclusively to literary works. (From now on I shall use this terminology throughout the book.) If we accept that the researcher must be located within the diagram, it is clear that there are only two basic positions which he can occupy: that of author, and that of reader (these are synonymous with sender and receiver respectively). There are many varieties of authors and readers and in later chapters I will look at some of the most important in detail but for the moment I shall concentrate on outlining the general features of the basic positions as they apply to researchers.

At various times we all occupy one or other of these positions. Often, as in ordinary conversation, we alternate rapidly between the two, talking and listening, or to put it technically, being the authors of a text then the readers of a text.

In a landscape, the position one occupies determines what one can and cannot see and what it looks like, so the first question to be resolved is, what is visible or hidden from each of the two basic positions?

Semiotic Positions

Figure 3.3

We are all the authors of texts; when we speak, write, paint, make films, or broadcast we take part in the making of texts. Sometimes we make texts in less obvious ways by our gestures, dress or even architecture, but all of these activities take place from a common point of view within the landscape of communication; as authors, we can see the texts we create but not their reading, which is always hidden from view:

> I'm not sure that this book does what it is supposed to do. I'm not certain that if you read it you will get everything out of it that I would like you to. But I guess that writers never really know if they are getting their points across. Wondering about it is a

gnawing kind of anxiety that I'm not used to and don't like. I
suppose that if lots of people buy a book, you can assume that
the few who first read it liked it and suggested that their friends
read it too. But you can never be sure if that's what's happening.
The people who read your book aren't around to tell you what
they think of it. In fact, they may be liking or disliking the thing
for all the wrong reasons. That's bewildering. It means, in effect,
that I don't really know what's in this book even though I've
been paying close attention to it for some time now. I'm not sure
I've managed what I was attempting here and I'm feeling a little
weird about it. (Tobey 1975, p. 13)

This extract comes from the opening chapter of a gardening book,
Pirating Plants, and straightforwardly captures a profound insight
about communication. At the heart of communication lies a
paradox: the text both joins and separates authors and readers.
Texts are like rivers in a landscape; they both join and separate the
opposite banks.

The gardener's plain admission of doubt also reveals another
basic insight about the process of communication. The text in the
reader's hands is not necessarily the same as the author's. This
suggests that we need to completely re-think our diagrammatic
representation of communication, for now instead of one text we
are faced with the possibility that there may be at least two. (Fig.
3.4)

Figure 3.4

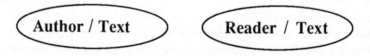

We must be clear about the sense in which there might be two
texts. Authors and readers may be confronted with the same
physical object; the book which leaves the writer's desk or the film
which leaves the studio may be physically indistinguishable from
the reader's copy or print. But in communication, as we saw with
the misleading electronic analogy, we are not concerned primarily
with physical characteristics but with problems of understanding.
We cannot be certain that understanding will be shared, that reader

and author will notice or pay attention to the same aspects of a text. To emphasise this possibility of difference, I am starting from the assumption that there are two separate entities — author/texts and reader/texts. It is always possible to modify this extreme scepticism in the light of specific evidence that on a particular occasion authors and readers share similar understanding. However, if one begins from the assumption that both authors and readers are confronted by the same object, it is much more difficult, as the history of semiotics shows, to admit the possibility of different understandings — different readings of the 'same' text.

If we now look at the author's position from this sceptical viewpoint we can see that any statement he makes about readers must be a construction — imagined — and any notion of the readers which he uses either implicitly or explicitly to guide the construction of his message must also be imagined. This needs to be understood as a general condition of communication, not as a communication failure that can be put right by replacing imagination with knowledge — as if there was some method by which authors can be brought closer to their readers. The author's view can never be the same as the reader's in the same way that the view of a mountain from the south can never be the same as the view of the mountain from the north.

Projection

As I suggested above, the separation of the author from the reader is not an unusual occurrence but the normal condition for communication. But as I have also shown in earlier sections *the author always creates an image of a reader; similarly the reader creates an image of an author.* These are the defining characteristics of the process of communication.

There are a variety of ways in which it is possible to describe the construction of readers by authors and vice versa. I have in my own research used the idea of an inferred reader or author (Sless 1980a,b, 1981a,b, 1983a). But there are some disadvantages with using the idea of 'inference'. It implies that authors or readers arrive at a view of their absent counterparts by a process of reasoning and this is misleading. It is certainly the case that readers or authors over time can change their mind about the nature of the other through inference but communication begins by *putting into*

a message some notion of a reader or author, and it is not necessarily the case that this *putting in* involves any kind of reasoning.

In order to give a clearer sense of what is involved I have gone
back to an idea which was developed by Ernst Gombrich in his
masterful study of the psychology of pictorial perception *Art and
Illusion* (Gombrich 1968). Gombrich shows that understanding
pictures does not simply depend on taking in what is in the picture.
Pictures are not self-evident. Each artist or viewer brings preconceptions which he or she imposes on the picture in the process of
making it, or in order to read it — an extension of what Gombrich
calls 'the beholder's share'. Gombrich cites the Rorschach inkblot
test as an instance in which the beholder's share is singled out for
special attention. But it is always there whether or not we

Figure 3.5: Ink Blot

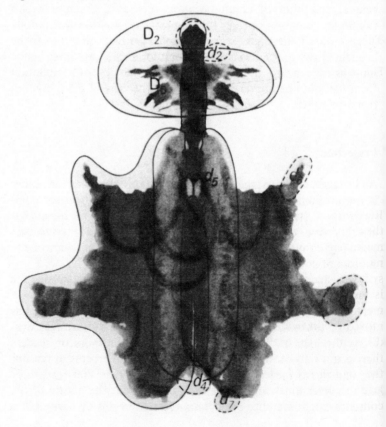

acknowledge or notice its presence. Gombrich is drawing on a deeper philosophical point first articulated by Kant, that all experience is an amalgam of prior conceptions and present information. Gombrich, borrowing an optical metaphor used by Rorschach, argues that the beholder *projects* his or her preconceptions on to the picture and out of this comes the reading of the picture.

Gombrich's preoccupation is with pictures as a particular kind of message or text. Our preoccupation is much broader and is concerned with how we read texts of all kinds, but the idea of *projection* is well suited to our needs. A condition of something being a text is that an author or a reader *project* on to it their absent counterpart. This is clearly understandable in the case of miracles or unusual astronomical observations; it is also clear that the gardener's doubts are about the shape and form of his projection.

The Reader's Position

Figure 3.6

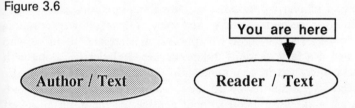

Readers *project* an author onto their engagement with the text but they can never see the author. The author exists only through the medium of the text. There is a parity on both sides of the communication process and the general conditions on either side are symmetrical with respect to each other. This means that the reader is, in an important sense, isolated from the author and any statement he makes about the author must be a projection. We have moved away from the electronic metaphor to something quite different. In the chapters to come there will be much to say about these projected entities. They act as a grid which viewers impose on the communication landscape stretching out before them and the grid recedes into the distant and unknown landscape defining the contours of the terrain which is hidden from view. According to our new metaphor, the student of communication is located in a landscape. This contrasts with the electronic metaphor which locates the student outside like a god. In the study of communication there is no omniscient vantage point from which all things are visible. We cannot look down from heaven and see everything. In communications research and, as I shall demonstrate, throughout semiotic research we are earthbound. We can see what is before us but we cannot see round corners or through obstacles.

Communication and Semiotics

We can now integrate the ideas in this chapter with the notions of semiotics developed in Chapter 1. Of first importance in semiotic research is an appreciation of the position of the semiotician within the logical web of communication and semiosis. Unfortunately, as I discovered, texts on the subject say very little about this. The imperialism of semiotic ambitions, the vision of a theory embracing the entire universe of semiosis, has led to delusions of grandeur, a sense of scholarly omnipotence. Describing semiotics as a science, as some of its founders did — and some of their followers continue to do — gives the subject a spurious prestige and to those who studied it a false sense of independence; semioticians, along with others interested in communication, implicitly assumed scientific objectivity, taking on board the ideas of communication as both sharing and transmission without considering the implications of these simple ideas.

But semiotics is not a science, it is something quite different. As I showed in the last chapter, human communication cannot be studied from an outsider's position of neutrality. Communication is a part of the universe of semiotic phenomena. Within communication there are two kinds of semiosis, one within the author/text relation and the other within the reader/text relation. We can see these two as complex mixes of the sign/user/referent relation of semiosis and we can also see that conducting semiotic research is itself an act of semiosis. This inescapable interweaving of subject and object requires us to turn to a new kind of research question. Traditionally the researcher as reader asks 'What am I studying?'. We must now augment this question with another — 'From where am I conducting my study?'. In the next chapter we will turn to a detailed answer of this question and find out what position the reader occupies in relation to the study of text. We are like the figures in a landscape: we can see only what is before us and must imagine what is hidden from view; our position in the landscape gives each of us a singular view though we share a common set of conditions. In the next chapter I shall explore the consequences of these common conditions.

Summary

Sharing is not an inevitable consequence of communication nor is it a defining characteristic of the process. However, a belief in sharing is essential, so too is the *projection* of authors or readers by their absent counterparts. Communication is broken into author/texts and reader/texts and researchers *must* occupy one or other of these positions. Researchers are like figures in a landscape: what they see depends on where they are standing.

4 READING POSITIONS

What is important, then, is less to decode what is said than to understand who is speaking to whom. In the field, the ethnographer is himself involved in the speech process and is just one speaker among others.

(Jeanne Favret-Saada 1980)

Introduction

Semiotics has been waiting in the wings for a long time; its entrance onto the centre of the intellectual stage is the product of a change in our world which has been gathering momentum since before the beginning of the industrial revolution. The very first mass production process was, if we use contemporary jargon, an information technology: it was the printing press. The growth of literacy and the development of modern communications technology has transformed our everyday experience. Texts (in the general sense in which I have used the term) have become a significant part of the human environment. We now spend a large proportion of each day surrounded by texts. At one time it might have been argued that we communicated in order to find out about the world but today we might suspect that communication is in itself an important part of the world; for it is not only an instrument through which experience is mediated, it is itself an experience. We may watch television news in order to find out what is going on in the world or read a book in order to increase our knowledge but we also indulge in these activities for themselves. We know what it means to curl up with a good book, watch the telly or go to the movies. These are experiences in and for themselves and in contemporary society they make up a substantial proportion of our everyday life. The mass media, which command so much of our time and attention, have become important sites of political and ideological struggle. At work, the nature of employment is changing; traditional manufacturing industries are declining, fewer people are directly involved in making things, and increasingly those in employment are concerned with the management or movement of information. Thus in leisure, politics and work, communication has assumed greater

significance. The emergence of semiotics as a contemporary intellectual interest is therefore not surprising. An important part of our
civilisation has developed and grown, and it needs to be explained
and understood.

As the last chapter will have made clear our relation to the multi-
picity of texts that surround us is by no means straightforward. We
cannot examine our relation to these texts as though we were
studying the climate or the flora and fauna of our environment.
Our relation to texts is special. Unfortunately semiotics has taken
the commonly available ideas of communication as sharing or as
transmission and developed its methods of research as if it was a
science.

The uncertainties which are part of any area of study are, in
semiotics, uniquely bound up with the all-pervasive process of
semiosis. Texts, by their very presence, demand understanding,
invite interpretation. We are always caught up in our own powers
of imagination and invention. Like Moses before the burning bush,
we create our gods, devils, friends and foes out of flickering forms.
There are no neutral positions, no places on the outside from which
to look in. The student of texts is a reader of texts. To recognise
something as a text — to even suspect that it might be a text — is to
bring semiosis into play.

We cannot see into texts or beyond them as if they were crystal
balls, oracles or cryptographs. There is, as this chapter will reveal,
an intellectual arrogance in stating, say, that it is possible to
discover what forces manipulate and control society by applying
invented categories to the reading of texts. To claim that texts, if
'read correctly', can reveal the structure of the human mind or the
dominant beliefs in a society is not unlike claiming to be able to tell
the future by reading tea leaves.

What follows in this chapter is an attempt to dispel both
arrogance and blindness by revealing the positions from which it is
possible to read texts. The scope of the semiotic vision is breathtaking in its scale, and the first lesson of the semiotic method
should be humility in the face of something much greater and more
complex than oneself.

Semiotics and Popular Culture

I could choose many kinds of critical writing to demonstrate the special relations between readers and text but there is some point in choosing work which has its roots firmly within a particular strand of semiotic inquiry; it allows us to link the ideas in this text to the tradition which precedes it, and we can then demonstrate why earlier work is inadequate and its findings need to be qualified.

Over the last 20 years there has developed a new radical and controversial interest in popular culture in which traditional semiotics has played a significant role. The origins of this contemporary intellectual concern are closely related to the highly visible growth of mass media and marketing in the post-war period. By the 1950s social critics of both the left and right were expressing alarm and concern about what seemed to them an undesirable increase in the power and influence of the mass media. To some, such as Vance Packard and Daniel Boorstin in the USA, it seemed that traditional values and notions of honesty and truth were being eroded by economic greed and political and editorial opportunism. In their view people were gullible, vulnerable to the persuasive powers of unscrupulous editors, unprincipled politicians and immoral but scientifically controlled advertising (Packard 1957; Boorstin 1962). To others, such as Richard Hoggart, it seemed that a whole way of life among the English working classes was being undermined by popular magazines and literature (Hoggart 1957).

Popular culture, traditionally despised as inferior to great literature and art, became an object of fascination and genuine interest in itself. But what characterised all the works mentioned above was the use of traditional forms of scholarship or journalism. None of them offered new ways of studying this emerging social phenomenon.

More thoughtful theorists, such as Raymond Williams, who concerned themselves with the overall direction of this emerging intellectual interest, warned of the dangers of approaching popular literature from the perspective of the literati (Williams 1958). But underlying this warning is a more general and regrettably ignored caution: imposing a particular viewpoint on the world, whether political or intellectual, is an act of imperialism; there is something wrong in trying to understand anything without first establishing the position from which one is conducting the inquiry. Unfortunately, the critics' desire to understand this new phenomenon was not guided by a sense of place or modesty. Popular culture was, in their eyes, a phenomenon of mass society, therefore it needed to be explained by theories which could accommodate such a scale. Far from questioning the legitimacy of their own elitist position, the new critics of popular culture looked for ideas that would enable them to see the social landscape from an even greater height. Semiotics, in a form generated by the French critic Roland Barthes, seemed to offer a new perspective and a new way of understanding popular culture.

Barthes' 'Mythologies'

Published originally in 1957, *Mythologies* has been the single most influential text directing studies in popular culture, particularly in England where, under the intellectual guidance of Raymond Williams and Richard Hoggart, Cultural Studies or Communication Studies (as it is now known) has become part of academic teaching and research. There are more substantial works by Barthes and others but *Mythologies* is one of the earliest and by far the most intelligible, evocative and entertaining. Barthes' writing is a masterpiece of rhetoric and grows out of a deep mistrust of French bourgeois society. The book consists of a collection of discrete essays which, with the exception of the last, are short critical review articles exploring the meaning of objects of popular culture in France, illuminating the commonplace in ways seldom realised by other critics. Barthes offers readings of such objects (or 'texts') as washing powder, margarine, motor cars and newspaper reports and demonstrates convincingly that these humble objects can be used to conjure up a world of myth and paradox. As, years ago, I read each essay for the first time, I was left with the compelling feeling that I had been shown a new way of looking at the world, a way of understanding texts with new meaning. Indeed part of the excitement of that first encounter was engendered by the implication running throughout the essays that objects previously ignored could be made to yield up a rich harvest of understanding and insight.

I have deliberately given a personal account of my first encounter with Barthes' work because, as I have been arguing, it is important to acknowledge that reading is a special kind of relation. I do not know how others read *Mythologies* but I believe that my own experience was probably shared by many people when they first encountered the work and it gives some idea of why it has proved to be so influential. It seemed from my position as reader to offer a new technique of social criticism.

But I was afflicted with a doubt about the generality of Barthes' method, a doubt which has grown over the years and caused me to re-read these sparkling essays from a new position, and to ask questions about the position from which Barthes seems to be talking about French culture.

In the final summarising essay, and elsewhere, Barthes explained that his method was to focus on the structure of texts. In a later essay on photography, he articulates this structuralist emphasis with reference to the idea of communication as transmission:

> The emission and the reception of the message both lie within the field of sociology: it is a matter of studying human groups, of defining motives and attitudes, and of trying to link the behaviour of these groups to the social totality of which they are a part. For the message itself, however, the method is inevitably different: whatever the origins and the destination of the message, the photograph is not simply a product or a channel but also an object endowed with a structural autonomy. Without in any way intending to divorce this object from its use, it is necessary to provide for a specific method prior to sociological analysis which can only be the immanent analysis of the unique structure that a photograph constitutes. (Barthes 1977, pp. 15–16)

Clearly Barthes is using the transmission idea of communication which has its origins in telecommunication. This is clearly shown (signalled!) by his use of terms such as 'emission', 'channel' and 'reception'; but further he also accepts that it is possible to separate the text from its relations with authors and readers so that it can be studied independently, albeit as a prelude to sociological analysis. Significantly, the way in which he describes the reading of texts is quite different from his description of studying them: 'reception of the message' is contrasted with 'the immanent [meaning inherent] analysis of the unique structure that a photograph constitutes', and it should not go unnoticed that the former sounds prosaic and passive, while the latter sounds academic and active. Barthes sees himself as operating *outside* the process of communication, not a reader but an observer. Ordinary people simply receive messages but semioticians conduct immanent analyses of their structure!

Returning to the essays in *Mythologies*, it should be possible to observe this curious detachment at work. We would expect to find the essays devoid of any comments about the reception or transmission of messages, concentrating entirely on the 'immanent analysis of structure' of the text. But what we actually discover is quite different. His essays are populated by the very people (that is, the public, the readers of the 'texts') he seeks to exclude.

The World of Wrestling

True wrestling, wrongly called amateur wrestling, is performed in second-rate halls, where the public spontaneously attunes itself to the spectacular nature of the contest, like the audience at a suburban cinema. Then these same people wax indignant because wrestling is a stage managed sport (which ought, by the way, to mitigate its ignominy). The public is completely uninterested in knowing whether the contest is rigged or not, and rightly so; it abandons itself to the primary virtue of the spectacle, which is to abolish all motives and all consequences: what matters is not what it thinks but what it sees. (Barthes 1977, p. 25)

The Blue Blood Cruise

Ever since the Coronation, the French had been pining for fresh news about royal activities, of which they are extremely fond; the setting out to sea of a hundred or so royals on a Greek yacht, the *Agamemnon*, entertained them greatly. (Barthes 1977, p. 32)

Throughout these passages there are explicit references to the audience which variously 'attunes itself', 'waxes indignant', is 'uninterested', 'abandons itself', 'pines' and is 'entertained' — a veritable sociology of the French public. These are among the more obvious references to the 'reception of messages' in the self-styled 'immanent analysis'. A close inspection of all the essays reveals the presence of audiences or authors — the ingredients of the communication process which are supposed to be omitted as independent of structure. Receivers of messages are not always so blatantly present: their *projections* sometimes lurk like shadows which can only be glimpsed as one passes through, but they are *never* absent. The reasons for this have already been indicated in Chapter 3 and will become even more apparent presently; what needs concern us here is the position from which Barthes seems to be speaking.

By what right does Barthes set himself up to pronounce on the attitude of a people? What special position does he speak from which enables him to indulge in such grand gestures? At stake is not whether his view is plausible or indeed whether he is right or wrong, but whether his position enables him to hold such a view without challenge. Clearly it does not. No one attending a wrestling match or following reports of royal occasions in the press can, without a great deal more information, even begin to give an account of how people respond to these events, let alone comment on the responses of an entire nation. Barthes' position is false. His reading of a text, however skilful or imaginative, does not allow him to do anything other than speculate on the behaviour of others. As he himself readily admits, the answer to these questions 'lies within the field of sociology'.

What, therefore, is happening in *Mythologies*? In the first place, Barthes is using the 'outsider's' rhetoric that I identified in the last chapter. The sad irony is that Barthes' critical rejection of French bourgeois values adopts the same imperialist posture that he finds so offensive in that class. Unfortunately, radical critics who followed Barthes' example also followed his style, and, as we shall see, this determined the direction of their work.

There is a second and more subtle answer to our question about *Mythologies*. As examples of the reading of texts they contain some of the ingredients which are basic to many reading positions and in the next chapter I will use these essays to begin the process of articulating the *actual* positions which a reader can take as opposed to the false positions that we have so far uncovered. Barthes was himself well aware of the paradoxical position he occupied, even if he chose to ignore it within the rhetoric of individual essays. This is very clear in some of his later writing, in which he shows a fascination with paradox, but it must have also been evident to him on completion of *Mythologies*, for in the preface he says,

> . . . what I sought throughout this book were significant features. Is this a significance which *I* read into them? In other words is there a mythology of the mythologist? No doubt, and the reader will easily see where I stand. But to tell the truth, I don't think that this is quite the right way of stating the problem. 'Demystification' — to use a word which is beginning to show signs of wear — is not an Olympian operation. What I mean is that I cannot countenance the traditional belief which postulates a natural dichotomy between the objectivity of the scientist and

the subjectivity of the writer, as if the former were endowed with a 'freedom' and the latter with a 'vocation' equally suitable for spiriting away or sublimating the actual limitations of their situation. What I claim is to live to the full the contradictions of my time, which may well make sarcasm the condition of truth. (Barthes 1977, pp. 11–12)

Throughout his life, Barthes was lured by paradoxes and preferred to play with contradictions rather than resolve them. In his absence, his essays are more pliable; and — using a well-worn term — we will exploit them to begin the process of demystifying the reading position.

Summary

Semiotics has become important because in our civilisation communication has become a major activity. The growth of popular culture has provided a fertile ground in which semiotics can flourish. Through the early work of Roland Barthes, the idea of structural analysis is explored and found to be based on a transmission notion of communication. Structural analysis is not simply an investigation of the structure of texts, as it claims, but invokes projected readers and authors. Barthes seems to be aware of the paradox involved in his method but does not seek to resolve it.

To the highly literate observer there is always a temptation to assume that reading plays as large a part in the lives of most people as it does in his own. But if he compares his own kind of reading with the reading-matter that is most widely distributed, he is not really comparing levels of culture. He is, in fact, comparing what is produced for people to whom reading is a major activity with that produced for people to whom it is, at best, minor. To the degree that he acquires a substantial proportion of his ideas and feelings from what he reads he will assume, again wrongly, that the ideas and feelings of the majority will be similarly conditioned. But, for good or ill, the majority of people do not yet give reading this importance in their lives; their ideas and feelings are, to a large extent, still moulded by a wider and more complex pattern of social life. There is an evident danger of delusion, to the highly literate person, if he supposes that he can judge the quality of general living by primary reference to the reading artifacts.

(Raymond Williams 1961, p. 297)

Introduction

In the previous chapter I focused on the presence of projected authors and readers in order to demonstrate that the purity of so-called 'immanent analysis' is asserted but never demonstrated. This assertion is a fundamental ingredient of structuralist semiotics (so called because of its emphasis on structure) but, as I shall demonstrate many times, there can be no reading of any text which does not entail bringing into existence these or similar projected beings. In the first instance I shall use material from the beginning of the structuralist era, before this simple fault became overlaid with spurious technicalities and the obvious became buried in obfuscation. I will then show with reference to more ancient and more modern work how these projected beings play a crucial role in the structuring of texts.

My argument is similar to, though much simpler than, the argument developed by Kant in his *Critique of Pure Reason*, where he shows that pure reason without preconception is impossible and that those who try to develop pure reason are deluded. A sense of the similarity in our projects can be evoked by using one of Kant's most luminous metaphors in which he likens the searchers after pure reason to a yearning dove.

> The light dove, cleaving the air in her free flight, and feeling its resistance, might imagine that its flight would be easier in empty space. (Kant 1781, tran. 1929, p. 47)

The 'air' of pure thought is preconception — Kant's *a priori*; the 'air' of pure structural analysis is the reader or author — real or projected. In the end structuralism is a false method. But ironically, and despite much of the damage which still lingers on in Cultural Studies caused by this false method, it produced an extravagant flowering of ideas about readers and authors. We can now map out the reading positions which structuralism tried so hard to ignore.

Unpacking Reading

Reading is a commonplace activity which we often take for granted. It is, however, the end product of an extremely long process of cultural accretion and individual learning. Centuries upon centuries of work has led to the varieties and kinds of texts that we ordinarily encounter. Within a single lifetime we all accumulate many layers of skill and knowledge, though when we read it seems like a simple act — one of understanding what is before us. We ordinarily think nothing of this densely packaged heritage. But in order to understand the place we occupy as readers we need to unpack the reading process — unfold some of its convolutions — so that we can be more critical of how it is used.

It is not possible to unpack the reading process all at once. As with a landscape, we cannot get to know it at one glance; it must be explored throughout its length and breadth, and through the seasons, before we can say that we know it. We should not expect a process which has accumulated for so long to reveal itself on first inspection. Barthes provides us with an excellent vista from which to plan our exploration.

The Romans in Films

In Mankiewicz's *Julius Caesar*, all the characters are wearing fringes. Some have them curly, some straggly, some tufted, some oily, all have them well combed, and the bald are not admitted, although there are plenty to be found in Roman history. Those who have little hair have not been let off for all that, and the hairdresser — the king-pin of the film — has still managed to produce one last lock which duly reaches the top of the forehead, one of those Roman foreheads, whose smallness has at all times indicated a specific mixture of self-righteousness, virtue and conquest. (Barthes 1957, p. 26)

As a reader of the above passage I can just glimpse the contours of a vast landscape stretching out before me. In the immediate foreground dominating my view is the passage written by Barthes. I cannot of course see Barthes but I can easily project his presence and guiding influence on the shaping of the text before me. Out of view, but imaginable from the lie of the land is the film of *Julius Caesar* by Mankiewicz. Experience tells me that beyond the film lies a vast and complex landscape taking a route via Shakespeare back to ancient Rome. (None of this is present to the eye, yet I assume it is there, below the horizon.)

If I take the reading position which Barthes seems to be offering me, then my gaze must come to rest on what is in fact out of sight. In this passage Barthes seems less preoccupied with projected readers but is giving me a glimpse of his projected authors. These authors are as out of reach to Barthes as he is to me yet he constructs a story — invokes their presence as authors — which through his own writing he passes on to me. It is a strange tale in which the studio hairdresser, armed with comb and curling tongs, mans the studio gates inspecting the cast for baldness.

Readers too are present but they take a shadowy form, like a blanket of cloud across the sky. Barthes tells me, as part of his story, that the size of Roman foreheads has 'at all times indicated' a certain meaning. This small phrase conjures up the vast legions of people who have ever gazed on a Roman forehead, who, according to Barthes, have responded in unison to the Latin brow.

If I alter my point of focus back to the immediate foreground I can see that part of my relation to 'The Romans in Films' involves my construction of Barthes as author. I have generated a construct by referring to his writing on photography and commenting on his work and influence. Thus when I refer to Barthes' reading of *Julius Caesar*, I am not referring directly to Barthes himself but to the projected author that I have generated. It is this projected author who then invokes the barber and the masses.

A Notation of Reading Relations

It should by now be clear that this short passage from *Mythologies* can be read in such a way as to unfold a whole pattern of projected relationships tightly packed within the reading of the text. As I will show, the same method of analysis can be applied to the reading of any text. But because these relationships can become quite convoluted and complex we need a simple notation by which we can represent them so that as the relations unfold we can keep track of them.

The first element in the notation must indicate my position as reader of a text. Reader and text form an indivisible unity — the reader/text relation. I shall refer to this unity as R0, so that whenever I use the symbol R0, this indicates, like the arrow on the underground map, I am here: I am reading a particular text, in this instance *Mythologies*. Next, I have to take account of Roland Barthes' relation to *Mythologies*, and once again we have the indivisible unity of author/text relation. I shall refer to this unity as A1. The number indicates the distance between me and the author/text relation. It is now possible to represent these two relations diagrammatically as in Figure 5.1. The dotted horizontal line indicates the imaginative link between me and the author of the text.

Figure 5.1

R0 .... A1

In order to incorporate Barthes' reading of *Julius Caesar* a further extension of the notation is necessary. Barthes is no longer an author but in this mode becomes a reader of a text. The notation can be extended so that Barthes becomes R1. By keeping the same number we can ensure that we know that this is the same identity (ie. Barthes) but in a different kind of relation. As Barthes is generating an imagined author from his reading of *Julius Caesar*, we need to extend the notation further. The author/text relation in this case becomes A2, and this can be added to the diagram above as in Figure 5.2.

Figure 5.2

$$R0 \ldots\ldots\ldots A1 \quad \vdots \quad R1 \ldots\ldots\ldots A2$$

The dotted vertical line between Barthes, the author of *Mythologies* and Barthes, the reader of the film *Julius Caesar* serves to delineate between the domains of these two texts, so that Figure 5.2 can be more clearly shown as in Figure 5.3.

Figure 5.3

Mythologies   Julius Caesar

$$R0 \ldots\ldots\ldots A1 \quad R1 \ldots\ldots\ldots A2$$

This diagram can now be expanded to include the play by Shakespeare on which the film is based.

Figure 5.4

Mythologies   Julius Caesar   Shakespear's Julius Caesar

$$R0 \ldots\ldots\ldots A1 \quad R1 \ldots\ldots\ldots A2 \quad R2 \ldots\ldots\ldots A3$$

It is clear how the diagram can be extended on the right as far as is necessary in order to include the full succession of author/texts and reader/texts which are incorporated in my reading of *Mythologies*. Notice that A1 and R1 are the same person or group acting as authors and readers respectively. The numerals 1, 2, 3 etc. are used to indicate the *distance* from me of the author/readers. Like any abstract notation system, the best way to understand it is to think oneself into its logic and apply it.

Beyond this first elaboration of the notation we need to consider a further feature of the communication process. In the extracts from *Mythologies* in Chapter 4, I pointed to the way in which Barthes conjures up projected readers through such phrases as '. . . the public spontaneously attunes itself to . . .', or '. . . the French had been pining for fresh news of . . .'. In 'The Romans in Films', the reference to projected readers is not so obvious but is none the less present in the phrase '. . . at all times indicated . . .'. This is apparent if we turn the phrase round and ask, to whom has the forehead indicated its meaning? Taken literally, Barthes is suggesting that the meaning of the forehead is universally recognised. These readers must be included in any representation of the communication process, but once we do so we begin to unfold a realm of complexity which is unsuspected in the commonplace process of reading.

From my position, Barthes' projected readers are greatly attenuated because for me Barthes is a projected author; I am therefore dealing with a projected reader constructed by a projected author. In other words, from my reading I infer that Barthes believes that other people will read in a particular way the texts he is discussing. None of this unfolding of projected readers and authors should be construed as questioning whether or not the projected entities correspond to actual authors or readers, which is a separate question outside our present concern, and in any case one which cannot be answered by a more careful or different kind of reading of Barthes' text. The process of analysis which I am outlining is concerned with unfolding the relationships which are to be found inside the process of reading. Barthes' projected reader of the film *Julius Caesar* can be represented as R1a in Figure 5.5.

In the last chapter I created a projected reader for Barthes' *Mythologies* by suggesting that I thought other people read the book in much the same way as I did. This too can be represented diagrammatically as in Figure 5.6.

Figure 5.5

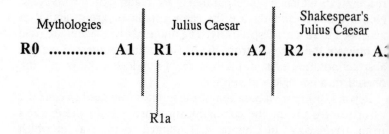

Figure 5.6

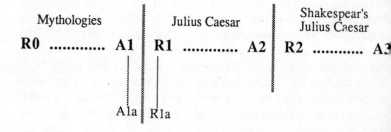

Our readings of texts are littered with these projected readers and authors. They are the fabric out of which we construct our understanding. As I have shown, there are many ironies attached to the structuralist project but none more so than the attempt to discover the structure of texts by ignoring the very entities which give them their shape.

Barthes' view became highly influential because it seemed to offer a new technique of social criticism, a view reinforced by the theoretical claims made in *Mythologies'* final essay (though his weak attempt at theory masked by obfuscation is not very successful). But the day is carried by one brilliant example. He describes a photograph on the front cover of *Paris Match* (Figure 5.7).

[A] young Negro in a French uniform is saluting, with his eyes uplifted, probably fixed on a fold of the tricolour.

It is, he argues, an image that carried all the connotations of French imperialism and the contradiction of the oppressed honouring the symbol of the oppressor, thus demonstrating how the system legitimises itself and at the same moment is made to reveal its contradictions. As an example of what he had striven to demonstrate throughout the book it seems impeccable and comes at the climax of the work. It is an image which often recurs in discussion of Barthes' contribution; yet there is a deep irony in that the photograph was not reproduced in *Mythologies*, and it is likely that most of the people discussing it have never seen it. Such is the power of Barthes' rhetoric, that the tricolour has been incorporated *into* reading of Barthes' image whereas in fact he tells us that the uplifted eyes were only *probably* fixed on the fold of the tricolour. Those in search of a new method of social criticism were easily satisfied by his reading of an image — his story of a reading — without wondering whether an alternative story could be told.

In general, the reading of texts entails the creation of either projected authors or projected readers. In some cases, as above, both are present. The variety of forms that these beings can take is, in principle, limited only by the imagination of the reader. In practice the limits are tied to the political and ideological outlook of the reader. Putting the matter very straightforwardly, *the projected readers and authors that we create depend on how we regard our fellow human beings.* In part, the structuralist fashion was politically very self-conscious in character. Yet it sought the political dimension of communication not in the relations between people and messages but in what it took to be the structure of messages. In doing this it unerringly ignored its own political view while ranging freely and imaginatively over what it took to be the hidden structure and shaping influence of ideology on other people's political views.

Now that I have elaborated the basic elements in my notation, we can use it to explore the variety of projected readers and authors that populate our reading of texts. The diagram in Figure 5.6 is not complete and the adventurous reader might take some delight in elaborating it further.

Other Readers

As I have shown, when we read we can pack many kinds of projected beings into the process; among these we frequently invoke

Figure 5.7

Front cover of *Paris-Match* no. 326. June 1955. 35 × 26·3 cm, original in colour. Photograph by courtesy of *Paris-Match IZIS*.

other readers. I have already mentioned my own and what I imagine are Barthes'. In general these other readers fall into two groups: those that are like us and those who are not. In my own case, as a reader of *Mythologies*, mine are clearly of the former kind; as I said, I thought my own experience was probably shared by others. Knowing that I was going to elaborate the ideas in this chapter, my remark in Chapter 4 was deliberately introduced, though when I first read *Mythologies* I was unaware of the intricate relations that could be read into the work.

We don't always have to search out the obscure interstices of critical writing to uncover the projected other readers, as they are sometimes quite clearly and explicitly visible. Nor do we have to search for these entities only in contemporary critical writing. If the principles that I am developing have any generality it should be possible to take any text, from any period, and discover these shaping shadows. In order to demonstrate my point, here is an extract from Plato's *Republic*, written in approximately 400 BC:

> Stories like those of Hera being bound by her son, or of Hephaestus flung from heaven by his father for taking his mother's part when she was beaten, and all those battles of the gods in Homer, must not be admitted in our state, whether they are allegorical or not. A child cannot distinguish the allegorical sense from the literal, and the ideas he takes in at that age are likely to become indelibly fixed; hence the great importance of seeing that the first stories he hears shall be designed to produce the best possible effect on his character. (Cornford 1941, pp. 68–9.)

Here we can discern an account of a reading that has echoed down the ages — its modern counterpart is to be found in the writing of those who advocate control of children's television viewing. The account it repeats is that, when reading messages, children fail to distinguish between fact and fiction and are thereby corrupted. The other readers in this case are children. The relations, which in this case are quite explicit, can be represented using my notation as shown in Figure 5.8. R0 is my reading of Plato. A1 is Plato as author of *The Republic*. R1 is Plato reading the stories of Homer and R1a is Plato's projected other readers of Homer — children. It is quite clear that Plato regards these other readers as different from himself.

The modern inheritors of Plato's paternalism are likely to invoke scientific detachment and claim that their view is objective; as scientists they observe texts while others — whether children, the masses or any other category — read texts. We have already seen how Barthes clearly distinguishes between 'receiving messages' and 'analysing their structure' and his attitude is one that is readily recognised and accepted in our society as an ordinary scholarly

Figure 5.8

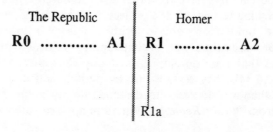

convention: the objective outsider. But as I have shown above, there is no outside position from which to observe a text; texts can only be texts if there are readers or authors. Scholars or scientists, to maintain the illusion of detachment, have to create projected readers who can take their place and whose reading they in turn observe. This curious convolution does not lead to objectivity as is supposed but in fact results in an obviously invented reading because the effort after detachment necessitates the creation of a projected being who would otherwise not exist.

In the case of Plato there is no doubting the profoundly political motives behind the control of children's reading; the children he was concerned with were destined to become the model rulers of society. Accounts of reading are politically motivated even when they do not obviously seem to be; they are never neutral or disinterested. The scientist wishes his view to prevail and so does the scholar, judge and critic. It is not in their interest to be wrong or to have someone disagree with them. Providing an authoritative reading of a text which plausibly invokes the responses of another reader gives the authoritative reader power over the other. We recognise this exercise of power most clearly among those who seek to control which texts we read and how we should read them, usually doing so from a position of supposed or real superiority; but another way of trying to exercise this power is by claiming that one's reading is the same as everyone else's. My next example is of this kind.

Judith Williamson, following Roland Barthes but with a much more elaborate array of structuralist and post-structuralist concepts, introduces *Decoding Advertising* to the reader in a foreword which closely parallels Barthes' personal declaration in the preface to *Mythologies*:

This book deals with a public form, but one which influences us privately: our own private relations to other people and to ourselves. . . . [T]o form a *theory* of advertising . . . breaks through the isolation of individual struggle. It can help to put personal reaction on a scientific basis, and its very impersonality is what validates the particular. (Williamson 1978, p. 10)

The struggle to elevate reading into observation is very clear in this passage. From other statements made in her foreword there is no doubting Williamson's commitment to a radical Marxist political position. She, like Barthes, is not pretending that she is politically neutral; and, like Barthes, she is caught in a contradiction of her own making. For on the very next page, in the introductory chapter, she says about advertising that

It is not my purpose here to *measure* its influence. To do so would require sociological research and consumer data drawing on a far wider range of material than the advertisements themselves. I am simply analysing what can be *seen* in advertisements. (Williamson 1978, p. 11)

How clearly this echoes the position taken by Barthes — and with much the same consequences. There is no doubt that some things can be *seen* in advertisements (though whether it is simple is debatable) but by *whom*? Williamson distinguishes between herself as 'simply analysing what can be *seen* in advertisements' and others whose reading can be determined by 'sociological research'. This parallels Barthes' distinction between himself as 'analysing [messages'] immanent structural properties' and other readers as 'receiving messages'. However, having made the distinction, Williamson dissolves it by incorporating all other readings into her own. This is accomplished by the simple device of using the plural 'we' or 'our' whenever she is explaining her own reading. Thus *we* share with her the reading of specific advertisements:

[T]he words and pictures catch *our* attention by their incongruity: *we* are drawn in, by attempting to understand the 'contradiction'. (my italics, Williamson 1978, p. 84)

or *we* find ourselves in the same sociological milieu:

Advertisements are one of the most important cultural factors moulding and reflecting *our* life today. (my italics, Williamson 1978, p. 11)

Thus her reading of advertisements becomes 'ours', as readers of her book. I would not doubt that advertising is in some sense important in our kind of society but how important and to whom seems to me an open question which cannot be answered by such a blanket statement. Certainly advertising is very important to Judith Williamson and her point of view offers a rich and fascinating insight into how a set of abstract concepts can be used to generate great meanings from meagre material. But her attempt to generalise her own experience to everyone else is in the end not scientific, as she claims, but an act of political rhetoric; she is trying by a process of persuasion to convince her readers of the correctness of her own point of view. Her method of trying to achieve this, as one last example will show, is by frequently incorporating us as readers of her text into her own reading by the simple device of using the word 'we'.

In an advertisement, we are told that we *do* choose, we *are* free individuals, we have taste, style, uniqueness, and we *will act accordingly*. In other words, having been attributed with the qualities connected with a product, we are projected as buyers of it, precisely because 'given' that we 'have' the beliefs implied in the ad, we will act in accordance with them and buy the product that embodies those beliefs. It is a sort of 'double-bind'. (Williamson 1978, p. 53)

Once again I find the delicious savour of Barthesian paradox. Williamson's 'we' is no different from her projection of the advertiser's projected readers. Thus a single double-bind becomes a double-double-bind. And two double-binds do not necessarily make a fact let alone a plausible argument! The irony of Williamson's position is that her own rhetoric must be at least as irresistible as she imagines the advertiser's rhetoric to be, otherwise not only does her argument become unconvincing but, by implication, advertisements may not be 'one of the most important cultural factors moulding and reflecting our life today'.

As the above rather convoluted argument shows, there is a weakness in Williamson's method; this can be seen more clearly if

Figure 5.9

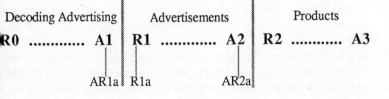

Decoding Advertising	Advertisements	Products
R0 .... A1	R1 .... A2	R2 .... A3
AR1a R1a	AR2a	

epresented using the notation (see Figure 5.9). Once again R0 represents my reading of a text; in this instance *Decoding Advertising*. A1 represents my projection of Williamson as author of the text and from this point in the diagram all references to Williamson are to my projection of Williamson. R1 is Williamson as a reader of advertisements. A2 is the advertiser as projected by Williamson and R2 is this projected advertiser 'reading' the product. AR1a is Williamson's projection of me as a reader of her text, based on her use of 'we'. R1a is Williamson's other readers for advertisements and finally AR2a is Williamson's projection of the advertiser's projected readers of advertisements. For Williamson's argument to be convincing it is necessary to assume that all the readers, with the possible exception of R2, will read the advertisement in the same way. Representing this relation formally using the notation would be as shown in Figure 5.10. It would only be necessary for one of these not to be equal to the others for the

Figure 5.10

$$R1 = AR1a = R1a = AR2a$$

entire argument to be in doubt. In other words the structure of the advertising message is *determined* by these shadowy presences, not by what can be 'simply seen' in the ads.

Conclusions

Readers of texts necessarily project beings which provide texts with their structure. In the case of readers who generate other readers, I have shown how these projected beings can be either like or unlike the reader who invokes them. In either case these beings are created in order to exercise control over actual readers and in this we begin to discover the close relationship between communication and power.

I have introduced a notation which can help to summarise and represent the intricate relations which are packed into the reading process. In future chapters there will be much more to say about readers — real or projected. In the next chapter I turn to a closer look at the peculiar quality of the projected authors in the reading of texts.

Summary

Pure structural analysis, such as that proposed by Roland Barthes in his early writing, is impossible as it ignores the existence of the reader who himself plays a role in the structure of texts. Any particular reading calls into being projections of other readers.

A notation system is described which allows the delineation of the many relations which exist between readers and their projections. The notation is used to demonstrate how multiple projections are conflated into a single reading.

6 VARIETIES OF PROJECTED AUTHORS

'The report of my death was an exaggeration.'
(Mark Twain, cable from Europe to Associated Press)

Introduction

In this chapter I shall continue unpacking the reading process, focusing on the projected authors that inhabit our reading of texts.

Anyone familiar with recent critical debates will be aware of the controversy which has attended the conceptualisation of authorship, and in part this chapter is indebted to that debate. But I shall not follow its tortuous path; rather I shall attempt to cut straight through to the issues so that the newcomer can gain an understanding of what is at stake without having to trace the steps of all those who have gone before. For the seasoned traveller, the consequences of this approach may well be bewildering; most of the familiar landmarks of the structuralist and post-structuralist debate will be ignored in favour of my own less convoluted style, reflecting in part my own position as a critical bystander rather than a participant in the recent extravagant logorrhoea. But one does not remain a bystander without reason and those reasons will become clear towards the end of this chapter.

Exploring the projected readers of texts is like unpacking or unfolding the convolutions of our cultural practices; by contrast, exploring and differentiating between the varieties of projected authors of texts is like exploding the reading process and at the same time disintegrating the text itself. Even the reader's position will not be untouched by such cataclysmic events. We must remember that the distinctive characteristic of semiotic relations is their interdependence; we cannot expect a change in ideas about the users of signs without it affecting our ideas about signs, referents and other users. The material and substantial world we take for granted in everyday life is no guide to what is fixed in the semiotic universe. As I shall show, all that remain stable are the *relations of semiosis* to which all communicative experience is bound.

Varieties of Projected Authors

The first kind of projected author is the one most of us would take to be the simplest kind: the individual, named author. In Chapter 3 I explored the assumptions and problems surrounding this privileged kind of projected author. Everything said there applies to other kinds of projected authors.

The second kind of projected author is what I shall call the social author. Judith Williamson's advertiser is such a social author. We think not of a particular individual as the author but of a role — someone who does a particular job, fulfils a particular function, or conforms to some stereotype: examples are newspaper reporter, bureaucrat, teacher and feminist. Though they may in fact be specific people in all their rich individuality, the reader's projection of them will only be as rich as the reader's conception of the particular social role. If a reader believes that advertisers are basically dishonest people who prostitute their talents to the whim of the highest bidder, then this will determine the way in which the reader will approach every advertisement. How we read the texts into which we project particular social beings depends very largely on the kind of people we think inhabit that social position.

The move from individual to social role is sometimes accompanied by a shift from a single text to a reading across texts. Thus Williamson is not concerned with the single advertisement but with the 'world of advertising'. Many such worlds have been created. The term 'genre' has been used to describe particular 'worlds' which (though it is often assumed that they have an existence of their own, and are treated as such) are in fact determined by projected authors and readers. Putting a text into the general category of fiction or, more precisely, into the category of comedy or black comedy invariably involves a complex of statements about how the text should be read, what the author might have intended, and whose style or previous work the author drew on. It is this web of projected beings that holds the text firmly, or sometimes loosely, within a particular genre, which means that genre can never be a precise or necessarily permanent category. As the critic's notions of projected authors and readers change, so will the definition of the genre or 'world' of the text.

The third kind of projected author is also social but in a different way. Many texts are the product of a collective enterprise; television and film, for example, are rarely if ever the product of a single individual. The normal modes of producing these texts involve a large number of people with different skills: acting, filming, sound recording, scripting, lighting, set designing, directing, producing and a great many other lesser known skills go towards making up the final product, so that it is impossible to say of any film or television programme that it had a single author.

The next plane of projected authorship involves a leap of imagination which takes us beyond the individual, beyond the group, even beyond specific institutions, to the level of culture. How can an entire culture be the author of a text? I shall answer this question by expanding the notion of this book's authorship in a series of stages so that at each point the reader can examine how the changed notion of authorship influences the reading of the book.

The obvious initial presumption is that this book is written by me, David Sless; certainly, a great deal of my time has been devoted to preparing the manuscript and reviewers would hold me responsible for its shortcomings. But there are other people — research assistant, editor, publisher, printer, binder — who have been responsible for producing the object which now sits in the reader's hands; it could be argued that this text is the product of a collective enterprise. If we look in another direction towards the influences which have shaped my ideas (even though I have kept the references to the extensive writing on semiotics out of the main body of the text), it is clear from an inspection of the bibliography that I am not an isolated thinker who has dreamt up this subject from his own imagination. I am situated within a debate and I am (or at least the part of me that wrote this book is) a product of that debate. And beyond semiotics lies the terrain of the English language in which this book was written. I was born into the community of English language users. I did not make the language but there is a sense in which it might be said that the language made me. It is therefore possible to see this book not as the product of an individual writer but the product of the discourse of semiotics which is in this instance located within and produced by the linguistic community of English speakers of which I am a part.

Examine at each stage of this expanding notion of authorship what happens to the reading of the text. At the first level of the individual author there is a sense of a psychological entity; this book can be compared to other writings by the same author Sless. Next, readers might locate the author within the milieu of a university. What you make of that will depend on the ideas you have of such a place and the people who work in it. From that vantage point the authorship of this book is located somewhere between the individual and the social author: a mixture of individual history and institutional role, and as such this book becomes comparable with other books produced within a similar milieu.

As the shift is made to the next level of authorship — the larger group — there is a tendency to examine other aspects which have previously been in the background. The reader can turn to the lay-out and typographic design of the book, the cover design, the proofing errors, any other books produced by the same publisher and so on. In the transition from one projected author to the next there is a change in foreground and background, a shift in attention from those features normally associated with individual authorship to a consideration of those associated with a new level of author-ship. Which elements become the focus of attention depends on the ideas and expectations we have about this new level.

Then we move into the discourse of semiotics, from which vantage point I am merely the confluence, the meeting point of dif-ferent ways of talking about a particular area of human interest. Semiotic discourse has arrived at a particular moment in its history which finds its expression through this book. I am the lens, not the light. Similarly, though not so obviously in this context, these notions of discourse can be extended to a more generally shared social experience; I am the site of intersection and struggle of a number of other discourses about gender, age, family, ethnicity, etc. This shift of attention places this book within an altogether new realm, where it is one instance among many of semiotic texts which collectively make up the semiotic discourse which have a special way of talking about the world. Now the kinds of questions which become relevant treat the text as representative of the semiotic discourse and at a more general level deal with the rules governing the formation of semiotic discourse. From this position the person, David Sless, is very much in the background — a product of the discourse, not a producer or even part-producer of a book.

Beyond the specific discourses is the language in which they are expressed and here too there is a shift in attention to the rules of the language of which this book and the semiotic discourse are merely an expression.

Authors and Ideology

Some readers may feel uncomfortable with the ideas I am developing because they do not accord with their expectations about the place of the individual in the world. Am I perhaps suggesting that the individual is of little consequence in the scheme of things? The transition from the individual projected author to the discourse is more than a change of level. What, I suspect, will disturb some readers is a more profound ideological move from a view of the world in which the individual's achievements, rights and interests are paramount to a view of the world in which the culture's production and collective activity is more important. On the other hand, some readers may welcome this shift as a release from our interest in self and the indulgence of individual interest at the expense of the group. The choice of level of projected authorship is not without its political or ideological import and this echoes my earlier observations about projected readers. We imagine the projected readers and authors that suit our ideological purposes.

Traditional forms of scholarship in areas such as art history or literature have been built around notions of individual authorship, valorising particular artists and writers and attempting to set them within a *background* of cultural influences. More recent critical practices have bypassed the individual and placed the culture in the *foreground*. The deliberate suppression of individual authorship among structuralist and post-structuralist critics is a reaction against the traditional scholar's relegation of social determinants and influences to a secondary position in favour of the celebration of the individual and hence an ideology of individualism.

We can get some sense of what is at stake through a particular example. Herbert Read, for many in the 1960s a significant figure in art criticism, was part of a community of scholars who articulated an ideology of individualism in which the artist was seen as hero. But even here, in the heartland of individualism, we can see the tensions between the individual and the culture. In Herbert Read's reading of *Les Demoiselles d'Avignon* — a painting by Picasso, the twentieth century's greatest artist-hero — we find the following:

. . . the main influence revealed in *Les Demoiselles* is Cézanne's. Picasso, like most artistic prodigies, was a roving eclectic in the early phase of his development. Influences from many sources appear in his work — Romanesque art of his native Catalonia, Gothic art in general, sixteenth century Spanish painting (particularly the work of El Greco), and finally the work of his immediate predecessors, such as Toulouse-Lautrec, and of the Fauves whom he met when he first settled in Paris. But these influences were comparatively sporadic and superficial: the influence of Cézanne was profound and permanent. (Read 1959, p. 68)

Through the work of an individual Read projects the work of other individuals and groups. It is as if Picasso was a battleground — a locus of struggle between conflicting interests out of which emerges the work. It would not take a great shift of emphasis or interpretation to see Picasso's *Les Demoiselles* as a product of a particular cultural moment rather than the work of a great genius. Once we follow this line of inquiry, the shift in emphasis is obvious. What becomes important is the place and time in determining the product, and the individuals, however talented, are swept along by the tide of events of which they are only a part.

But if ideological considerations about the nature of individuality are applied consistently to everyone, whether authors or readers, then the implications are much wider and more penetrating than re-directing the reader's attention away from the individual author and towards the social. For the voice that announces the death of the individual author in similar fashion dispatches the individual reader. As readers of texts we are the product of our culture; hence, if we accept the argument in its full form, we must not only preside over the funeral of the author but prepare the mass grave of individualism in all its forms. Thus when Judith Williamson confidently announces her ubiquitous 'we', she speaks as if from the grave-side of bourgeois individualism, celebrating the wake. From this reading position projected author and reader are homogenised through common cultural experience.

But is one person's reading of the culture as valid as anyone else's? Sharing, as I showed in Chapter 3, is more easily spoken about than demonstrated, and in the last chapter I showed how fragile Williamson's argument becomes if we cannot assume the *shared* basis of cultural experience. There are some other reservations and doubts about the form of this argument which need to be explored more fully before we can announce that life has departed from the individualist reader or author.

Killing the Author and Conquering the Text

One of the themes that runs throughout this book is my dislike of the intellectual imperialism of semiotics and my desire to evolve a semiotics that cannot take an imperial point of view. Ironically, a great deal of contemporary semiotic thought has been associated with fashionable radical dissent which has used the imperialism of capitalism, its cultural and ideological consequences, as a whipping boy and a scapegoat for the ills of our time. But imperialism is not exclusively a sin of capitalists: its roots lie much deeper. Conquering, subjugating and exploiting other people is an ancient practice and intellectuals have been at work for many centuries evolving ideas and ways of thinking to justify it. Nowhere is this more evident than in the intellectual traditions of European and North American thought where the intellectual enterprise has progressively asserted its authority over ever larger domains. As we move towards the close of the twentieth century the intellectual can claim, as at no other time, that he has dominion over every aspect of the world.

Semiotics has been part of this imperialist tradition and in many ways can be seen as part of its crowning apex. The writing which has inspired much of the current interest in the subject is, as I shall show in later chapters, pervaded with imperialist metaphors. Even when semiotics was adopted as part of a radical critique of capitalist modes of cultural production, the imperialist habit of mind asserted itself. The first victim of the war against the so-called cultural hegemony of the capitalist system was the author.

The treatment of the author by students of semiotics is loosely analogous to the treatment of Aboriginal society by the early white colonists. When the latter arrived in Australia they found a land already populated by an indigenous population. To assert title over the land the colonists found it convenient to regard the Aboriginal people as simple hunter-gatherers who lived off the land but did not cultivate it. To the Anglo-Saxon mind it seemed obvious that those who worked the land, making it productive, had a better claim to it than those who wandered over it picking up what was useful and moving on. (In fact the Aboriginal people did cultivate the land by systematically burning areas to encourage new growth, and had well-developed methods for looking after the environment.) What has happened to the Aboriginal people is a great tragedy, one that will strike a familiar chord in other parts of the world that have fallen under colonial power.

I would not suggest that the history of semiotics has such blood on its hands but the pattern of thought that legitimised the theft of Aboriginal property is analogously and quite clearly reflected in the way in which semiotics has sought dominion over that coveted item of intellectual property — the text. There are many ways of demonstrating this: I shall give one example from recent English critical writing on film which gives some insight into how the territory was claimed.

Film criticism is a relative newcomer; one of its earliest attempts to generate an intellectual style of its own was through what came to be known as *auteur* theory. This was a critical practice that put the director at the centre of attention and argued that a film was the personal expression of the director. It is easy to see that this idea was part of the long tradition of art criticism already mentioned, which valorises the unique creativity of the individual genius. Its roots are in romanticism.

Several criticisms are made about *auteur* theory which can be applied to all approaches that focus on the author. In the first place, film is rarely if ever the product of one individual and to concentrate on an individual inevitably means neglecting the social nature of film production. Secondly, by emphasising the individual, the culture in which the work was produced is neglected as a determining factor. Thirdly, the approach totally ignores the circulation and audience for the film which are also important in its critical appraisal. All these criticisms were well in place (Buscombe 1973), when, in the early 1970s, semiotics was introduced and with it came a radical annihilation of the projected author.

Whatever the position of an author might be, the struggle among the critics was over film — the new territory to which they had no automatic title but which they wanted to exploit. What better way to assert the authority and territorial rights of the critic than to dismiss the author's rights, asserting confidently that the author was a mere figure in the social landscape of film language with no more territorial claims than the noble savage has over nature.

> What can it mean, however, to speak of the author as a source of discourse? The author is constituted only in language and a language is by definition social, beyond any particular individuality. (Buscombe 1973, p. 87)

There is of course, as with all forms of imperialism, one rule for the exploited and another for the exploiter. The journal *Screen*, which championed the displacement of the author, applied a different rule to its own authors. Figure 6.1 below shows a typical extract from the journal's pages advertising available back issues.

Figure 6.1: Advertisement from *Screen*

SCREEN BACK NUMBERS

The following back issues are still available. For prices see p144

V15 N1, SPRING 1974   Fortini The Writers Mandate and the End of Anti-fascism; **Vaughan** The Space Between Shots; **Gardies** Structural Analysis of a Textual System

V15 N3, AUTUMN 1974   Eikhenbaum Problems of Film Stylistics; **Brik** Selected Writings; **Mulvey and Wollen** interview on *Penthesilea*

V15 N4, WINTER 1974/5: INNER SPEECH Willemen, Levaco on Eikhenbaum and internal speech, **Bordwell** on Eisenstein, **Bellour** The Obvious and the Code, on *The Big Sleep;* **Hanet** The Narrative Text of *Shock Corridor;* **Hoellering** interview on *Kuhle Wampe*

V16 N1, SPRING 1975   Heath Film and System — on *Touch of Evil* (1st part); **Ellis** on Ealing Studios

V16 N2, SUMMER 1975: PSYCHOANALYSIS SPECIAL ISSUE Metz The Imaginary Signifier; **Heath** Film and System (cont)

V16 N3, AUTUMN 1975   Mulvey Visual Pleasure and Narrative Cinema; **Bellour** The Unattainable Text; **Rose** on auto-visualisation and *Peter Pan;* **Branigan** The Point-of-view Shot; **Buscombe** on Columbia 1926-42; **Baxter** on film lighting; **Kuhn, Johnston** on feminist politics, criticism and film history

V16 N4, WINTER 1975/6: BRECHT EVENT EDINBURGH FILM FESTIVAL 1975   Heath From Brecht to Film; **Brewster** Brecht and the Film Industry; **MacCabe** on *2 ou 3 Choses* and *Tout va Bien;* **Mathers** on Brecht's theatre in Britain; **Johnston and Willemen** on the independent political film and *Nightcleaners;* **Pettifer** on *Mutter Krausens Fahrt ins Glück* and *Kuhle Wampe*, **Lovell** on Lindsay Anderson; **McArthur** *Days of Hope*

Source: From inside the front cover of *Screen*, spring 1979, Vol. 20, No. 1.

There can be no doubt that even while *Screen* proclaimed the universal death of the author, its own authors, in their full idiosyncratic individuality, were well looked after and very much alive. Not only do their names appear in bold type before the 'discourses' but in some cases the word 'on' leaves the reader in no doubt as to the 'particular individuality' who is the 'source of discourse'. Similarly, the front cover of the journal, unlike many more conventional academic periodicals, gives prominence to authors. My particular favourite is the spring 1979 issue, announcing:

Foucault/Clayton and Curling: Questions of Authorship

(There is a non-alcoholic drink called *Claytons*, marketed in Australia as 'The drink you have when you're not having a drink', and the term 'A Claytons' has become identified with all forms of false substitution. Perhaps the 'Clayton' referred to in *Screen* is the author you have when you're not having an author!)

Foucault's article on the 'author function' concludes:

We can easily imagine a culture where discourse would circulate without any need for an author. Discourses, whatever their status, form or value, regardless of the manner of handling them, would unfold in a pervasive anonymity. No longer the tiresome repetitions: 'Who is the real author?' 'Have we proof of his authenticity and originality?' 'What has he revealed of his most profound self in his language?' New questions will be heard: 'What are the modes of existence of this discourse?' 'Where does it come from; how is it circulated; who controls it,' 'What placements are determined for possible subjects?' Behind all these questions we would hear little more than the murmur of indifference: 'What matter who's speaking?' (Foucault 1979, pp. 28–9)

But even if it does not seem to matter who is speaking behind the questions, it still matters, as the editors of *Screen* realise, who is asking the questions — and one cannot ask questions without speaking.

The struggle for power over the text by warring critics is not unlike a contest between colonial powers over territory. Those claiming the gift of semiotics are merely the latest in a long line; their weapons may seem new but their objectives are the same. The projected author is merely another native victim of the struggle. The imperial critic has, however, made sure of his own authorial identity and survival in the battle.

Conclusion

The projected author of a text as viewed from the reader's position can take a variety of forms from the single individual to the whole society. Each form alters the nature of the reading of the text. The first task of those who want to exert control over how texts are read is to control the nature of the projected authors or readers and, as I showed in the last chapter, these projected entities provide a text with its structure.

One important consequence of focusing on the shifts in attention provoked by different projected authors is the realisation that underlying all reading processes there are certain regularities. Reading is not entirely a personal matter; we cannot make what we want out of any text. There are definite consequences attendant on different ways of reading.

Summary

The next step in unpacking the reading process is to examine the idea of projected authors. There are several different types of authors that readers project onto texts. The first is the individual — a particular person. The second type of projected author is social in the sense that instead of an individual person we think of a particular kind of person: for example a reporter, advertiser, father, etc. The third kind of authorship is collective: such as a film company, newspaper, publisher, etc. Finally there is the culture as author. Those who have championed the death of the individual author in favour of the culture have not been consistent and their inconsistency has revealed an important relation between reading and exerting power over the text.

7 DISAPPEARING AUTHORS

ALL ANIMALS ARE EQUAL BUT SOME ANIMALS ARE
MORE EQUAL THAN OTHERS.

(George Orwell 1951, p. 114)

Introduction

Semiotics deals with all kinds of *stand-for* relations, though so far I
have concentrated on those *stand-for* relations that are part of
communication. Through a number of examples it has become
clear that the defining characteristic of communication is the projection of authors and readers on to a text. Between the semiotics
of communication and all other semiotic phenomena there is a
transition zone in which projected authors fade away or disappear
and we move from communication to understanding in general. In
this chapter I want to trace some of the ways in which we allow
these projected entities to fade away.

In Chapter 5 I demonstrated how some ways of reading texts
compress certain projected readers into the convolutions of the
reading process, only to become visible once the process is
unfolded. In the last chapter I showed something of the variety of
different kinds of projected authors that can be used. These
projected entities are the forces that shape and power the reading of
the text. There are also, as I showed, some kinds of reading in
which the adoption of one kind of projected author has the effect
of squeezing out other authors from inside the folds of reading: the
individual author can be replaced by a variety of social authors
including the entire culture. I will now turn to some of the consequences of eliminating authors completely. Once I have exposed
the illusory practice of eliminating authors the way will be prepared
for developing the general theory of semiotics (of which the semiotics of communication is only a part). I will begin by examining
the recently-emerged field of discourse analysis for evidence of the
process of eliminating authors.

Delusions of Discourse Analysis

Recent years have seen the emergence of a new field of inquiry called 'discourse analysis'. Just as the microscope eventually gave rise to the study of microbes, so, in part, modern recording and transcription equipment has spawned the study of discourse by allowing the recording of the spoken word. But unlike the microscope which brought biologists closer to their objects of study, the tape recorder and the process of transcription have in fact distanced discourse analysts from their object of study.

Discourse analysts study many aspects of conversations, utterances and the comprehension of texts. There is no single theory or method of discourse analysis and, as must be obvious from the spread of its subject matter, no single theory is likely. But if there is any possibility of evolving a unifying set of ideas to embrace this realm, that possibility lies in semiotics. To give shape to that possibility I shall apply some of the simple ideas I have developed so far to one particular kind of discourse analysis: the study of spoken discourse.

In order to develop my argument I shall unpack the reading process undertaken by discourse analysts, applying the notation developed in Chapter 4, beginning, as all such use of the notation must, with my own position, R0. I am intitially concerned with my relationship to the body of ideas and ways of talking that collectively make up the practices of discourse analysis. I have chosen a particular text which seems reasonably representative of the current state of discourse analysis (Brown and Yule 1983).

It is apparent straight away that this enterprise is problematic. There is no simple way of ensuring that my account is what I claim it to be: all the problems of projected authors and readers which have so far been explored are applicable to this instance. The scholarly mode in which I seem to be operating allows me a privileged position that is potentially powerful because it implies that my reading of *Discourse Analysis* by Brown and Yule has been on behalf of you, my reader. In effect this implication, if spelt out, says that if you — my reader — were in my position, with my knowledge and understanding, you would read this particular text in the way that I have; I therefore assume the power of doing your reading for you. Unless I abandon the task before me there is no way I can disclaim this bid for power. I must minimally hope for some assent to my views otherwise this entire enterprise is pointless.

This much is tied irrevocably into the process of communication. As the reader of my text you are in principle free to dispute my reading at many levels; in this way the reader of a text is always freer than the author, even though, paradoxically, it is the author who seeks to control the reader. In communication, the first consequence of trying to control the freedom of other is the restriction of one's own.

The relations as I have so far explored them can be represented as shown in Figure 7.1. R0 is my position as reader of the text

Figure 7.1

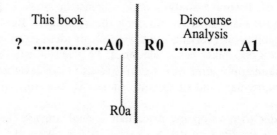

Discourse Analysis, A0 is my position as writer of this book, R0a is my projection of you the reader of this text on whose behalf I am reading the text on discourse analysis and finally A1 is Brown and Yule, not as individual authors but as representative of the community of researchers in this area of study. It is their discourse practice that interests me, not they as individuals. Notice particularly their representative function: within the web of relations that I have so far unfolded, the individual author/text relation *stands for* the discourse which is shared by a community of researchers. This places a burden of responsibility on the authors, which is rather different from killing them off or dispossessing them! I am treating them as representative ambassadors who are speaking on behalf of and in the language of all researchers in this field. There are obvious risks in such an appointment: the ambassadors may not be representative of their kind. But with all the risks and complexity that might be contingent upon their appointment, the act of making them *stand for* all others is itself simple, readily invoked and a demonstration of the way in which semiosis can occur at any level between two entities as long as there is someone there to

ctivate the process. One of the fascinations of semiosis is its end-
ess presence. The move from individual authors to the level of
ollective practice and belief, for all its attendant complexities, is
tself a simple *stand-for* relation.

Next in the process of analysis I move on to the text, *Discourse
Analysis*. It opens with the following statement:

> The analysis of *discourse* is, necessarily, the analysis of language
> in use. (Brown and Yule 1983, p. 1)

After some preliminary theoretical discussion in which different
iews of the purpose of discourse are raised and some general
emarks are made about the differences between written and
poken discourse, the text reveals that the opening claim is not
trictly speaking true.

> In general the discourse analyst works with a tape-recording of
> an event, from which he then makes a written transcription,
> annotated according to his interests on a particular occasion. . . .
> (Brown and Yule 1983, p. 9)

Thus Brown and Yule (speaking presumably on behalf of other dis-
ourse analysts) are not really analysing 'language in use' but
anguage taken *out of use* for purposes of analysis. But these are
ot unreflecting scholars, unaware of the problems they are
reating (even though they *are* illogical), for they say of the
iscourse analyst:

> In this creation of the written version of the spoken text he [the
> analyst] makes an appeal to conventional modes of interpreta-
> tion which, he believes, are shared by other speakers of the
> language.
>
> It must be further emphasised that, however objective the
> notion of 'text' may appear as we have defined it ('the verbal
> record of a communicative act'), the perception and interpreta-
> tion of each text is essentially subjective. Different individuals
> pay attention to different aspects of text. . . . In discussing texts
> we idealise away from this variability of the experiencing of the
> text and . . . take it for granted that readers of a text or listeners
> to a text share the same experience. (Brown and Yule 1983,
> p. 11)

There are several curious features in this argument. Mos
obviously there is a contradiction: either individuals read texts dif
ferently or everybody reads texts in the same way. It is not possible
however, to assert both of these propositions simultaneously. Eve
if we allow a weak sense of this proposition to remain, namely tha
some aspects of a reading are the same and others are different, w
are still left with the problems of deciding which aspects of
reading these are and, if the only instrument for discovering this i
reading, which reader is to undertake this task? It can only be
reader who 'shares the same experience' as other readers. Thu
everything is predicted on the assumption of sharing. There can b
no room in this scheme for misunderstanding or lying.

The theory of discourse analysis proposed here by Brown an
Yule does not abandon the presumed power of the omniscient out
side observer which I criticised in Chapter 3; it circumvents th
problem by allowing the observer to exert his authority fron
within. Thus the 'idealising' of reading is nothing less than decidin
on behalf of others what is or is not important to them.

The question which I am trying to probe is: what is the relation
ship between the analysts of discourse and the discourse they ar
analysing? I take this to be a specific case of the more genera
theme of this book. For me the text *Discourse Analysis* is litteree
with disturbing clues, as in the next quotation, which show hov
assumptions about sharing give rise to the illusion of bringing th
analyst closer to their subject but in fact drive the analysts furthe
away from the subject they are trying to investigate. As this nex
passage shows, even obvious evidence of a rupture in the smooth
coherence of mutual understanding does not serve to draw th
analyst back to a closer inspection of the original discourse bu
instead encourages the creation of a new discourse which is eve
further from the original.

From time to time however we are brought to a halt by differen
interpretations of 'the same text'. This is particularly the cas
when critical attention is being focused on details of spoke
language which were only ever intended by the speaker a
ephemeral parts, relatively unimportant, of the working-out o
what he wanted to say. It seems fair to suggest that discours
analysis of spoken language is particularly prone to over analy
sis. A text frequently has a much wider variety of interpretation
imposed upon it by analysts studying it at their leisure, tha

would ever have been possible for the participants in the communicative interaction which gives rise to the 'text'. Once the analyst has 'created' a written transcription from a recorded spoken version, the written text is available to him in just the way a literary text is available to the literary critic. It is important to remember, when we discuss spoken 'texts', the transitoriness of the original. (Brown and Yule 1983, p. 12)

Thus, when in doubt about interpretation, Brown and Yule do not return to the source, but create a new discourse. The new discourse is a discussion *about* spoken texts in which we *remember* the 'transitoriness of the original'.

The sense of distance of which I have spoken is seldom apparent because so much is squeezed out of the reading process but by using the notation I can give a better idea of what is involved. Figure 7.2 shows the simplest representation I can give of the unfolded process of reading from my position back to the spoken discourse which is the object of study. From this it can be seen that the discourse analysts are three times removed from their object of study. Two acts of interpretation have already taken place with all the attendant implications of projected authors and readers lying (perhaps in both senses) between the analysts and the discourse. It is very clear why so much hangs or falls by the analyst's faith in sharing. Such is the power of belief! Belief in sharing enables the analyst to squeeze out the intervening readers and authors and pretend that he is an analyst of discourse instead of a reader of a written text which is the result of two levels of interpretation of the original discourse.

There is something odd going on here that needs to be explored. It is important to realise at the outset that this method of study is not confined to the study of spoken discourse: television and film discourse is commonly studied in this way. Video or film sequences are reduced to story-board format where the sequence of script and visuals are placed alongside each other in written form for study. In all of these it must be the case that the further away one is from the thing one is studying, and the more stages of interpretation there are preceding the analysis, then the less likely is the analysis to be sensitive to the object of study. But the greater the distance, the more plausible the analyst's imaginative projections become and the greater is the vicarious power that the analyst exerts over the object of study, or as Brown and Yule define it, the 'data'.

Brown and Yule are at pains to point out that studying written

Figure 7.2

ext is no more objective than studying spoken discourse directly
ut if one looks closely at the specific ways in which they describe
heir relationship to what they are investigating, a different picture
merges. Thus in the extract above, analysts 'impose' interpreta-
ions and once texts are in written form they are 'available' to
hem. This is a language of authority, of power, not disinterested
cholarship. There are other indications in the Brown and Yule text
hat contradict the 'subjective' posture and suggest a dependence
n 'scientific objectivity'. They resort to the language of science to
egitimise the activity of discourse analysis.

> The discourse analyst is interested in the function or purpose of *a
> piece of linguistic data* and also in how that *data is processed*,
> both by the producer and the receiver. It is a natural consequence
> that the discourse analyst will be interested in the *results of
> psycholinguistic processing experiments* . . . (my italics, Brown
> and Yule 1983, p. 25)

Nothing more clearly suggests an objective scientific approach than
eferring to 'data', 'data processing' and 'experiments'; it brings to
mind an image of the scientist detached from and disinterested in
his observations. Ironically we find such a figure in the place where
he authors are most anxious to explain their sensitivity to the
context in which the spoken discourse takes place. Referring to
deas on how to 'investigate' context by one of the leaders in this
ield, they write:

> Hymes' features constitute essentially a checklist which would
> enable a visiting ethnographer to arrive by helicopter in a loca-
> tion where a communicative event is in process and to check off
> the detail of the nature of the communicative event.
>   Let us consider such an ethnographer as an invisible witness to
> a particular speech event. (Brown and Yule 1983, p. 39)

I find it difficult to conjure up the image of an ethnographer
dropping out of the sky without imagining less benign forces
swooping down in their choppers. If someone dropped in on me in
he middle of a 'communicative event' — whatever that might be —
I would find it very difficult to think of him or her as an ethnographer and if I happened to discover that my visitor had a way of
making him or herself invisible I would not jump for scientific joy

but would get extremely worried about the *power* which that gave him or her.)

What then is at stake in the distancing of the analyst from the spoken discourse? What the film, video and spoken discourse have in common is their transient quality. In that mode they cannot be controlled by the analyst. Necessarily the analyst must participate, accept the flow of time as a condition of inquiry and be *part of* the discourse. But from this position he has a limited authority over so-called data or knowledge. What the analyst seeks is not so much authority over people directly as over this curious commodity called knowledge. In order to transform experience, understanding and interpretation which he cannot completely control into this commodity called 'knowledge' which he can control, he has to distance himself from the former to a point where the influence of other participants can no longer be felt. This point can only be reached when the spoken discourse is transformed into written text, and the intervening authors and readers can be squeezed out of the frame of view so that the analyst can, as it were, see clearly through to the 'data'. From this position the analyst does not need to make any concessions of his powers to the process of discourse. He can avoid the questionable status of intruder and take on the authority of a sovereign; he can reign over text, dropping in out of nowhere to any point in the text, staying as long as he chooses and returning with his plunder without having to become involved. Yet it is a curious domain over which he rules because it is in fact largely made up of his own imaginings. He is reassured by his view that he is in the same position as the author whose discourse he has usurped, and so, while professing interest in others, he ends up by studying himself. This is the worst kind of solipsism because it deludes both the analyst and those who accept his view into believing that imagination is in fact knowledge gained by experience.

I would not suggest that the imagination of discourse analysts is of no value; if nothing else, they are thinking profoundly about the use of language and, however attenuated their experience, it adds to the stock of ideas and insights. But there is a price to pay for these particular insights which may cause us to question their value, for they are conceived in dominance bringing about either the elimination or the suppression of projected authors.

Disappearing Photographs

Exercising dominance involves suppressing or putting to one side a chain of projected authors. But suppressing authorship is not a practice confined to students of discourse; and in many instances it is an innocent practice, as I shall show with reference to our common habits of reading photographs. This will lead towards a clearer understanding of the difference between communicative and other kinds of semiotic phenomena.

Reading photographs is such a commonplace activity that even calling it reading seems supererogatory but as I have already shown with respect to reading other texts, the simple can often display a high degree of complexity once unpacked. The photograph in Figure 7.3 can be read in many ways. I shall consider a few of these.

Firstly, those with a knowledge of American art photography might recognise this image as one taken by the American photographer Edward Weston. Secondly, someone without the above knowledge but with a sensitivity to formalist aesthetics in the visual arts might read this as a well-composed formal photograph. Thirdly, someone without any of the above knowledge, but finding it in a specific context, such as a text on botany, could read it as an example of scientific photography. Finally, it may be read as a straightforward record of the appearance of the object which was in front of the camera. In each of these different readings it is possible to discern the presence or absence of different projected authors. In the first it is possible to discern the single named author, in this case an artist by social role, and therefore any notions the reader has about artists become part of the shaping of the reading of the image. The formal aesthetic reading embodies some notion of intent, which if not attached to a specific person, is at least seen as within the control of someone with a discerning eye for such formal considerations. To read the photograph as an image in a science text is to all but obliterate the photographer who is reduced to the level of an instrumental agent, much in the way that the person who records the spoken discourse is treated in the last example. Finally, if the photograph is read as nothing more than a visible record, then the photographer has disappeared completely from view. This final reading is particularly important at the moment because it marks the boundary between the semiotics of communication and the rest of the semiotic domain.

Throughout these different readings we can consider the

Figure 7.3: Photograph by Edward Weston

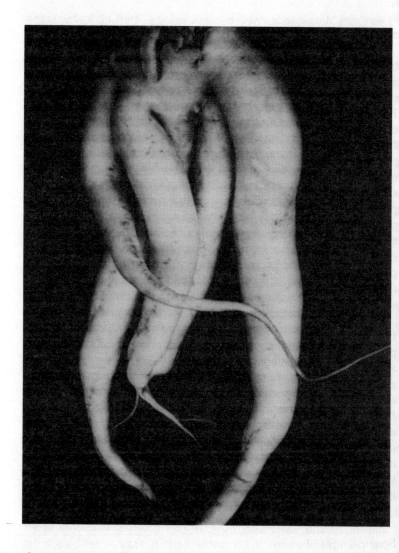

photograph as a sign, but in each case what it stands for is subtly inflected by the different projected authors. Reading a photograph as if it were a direct unmediated record of reality suppresses the presence of the author completely. It is no longer the product of somebody's efforts and decisions, it is simply a displaced part of the world. The relation between the sign (photograph) and its referent (plant root) seems to be causal; the photograph is purely the product of the physical laws of optics and photochemical effects.

The disappearance of the photographer and its implications can be demonstrated even more dramatically. The pages of this book and indeed most books produced today are the end product of a number of photographic processes. Even the photograph in Figure 7.3 is a copy of a photograph many times removed from the original; at each point there has been a guiding hand, an individual fulfilling a particular role, and, contrary to what might be supposed, decisions have been made at each of these points which do not necessarily transmit the image onto the next stage without in some way changing it. Anyone doubting this should compare the photograph above with other reproductions of this image and if possible with an original Weston print. At the final printing for this text, Figure 7.3 and the typeset script were pasted down onto the same sheet and together were photographed to make the plate for printing the page. The reader has been looking at photographs throughout this book, but only in the case of Figure 7.3 has the sense of a photograph been retained.

There are a number of reasons for this disappearing photograph. In the first instance the reader may be unaware of the technical processes that constitute book production, in which case the disappearance is due to lack of appropriate knowledge. But the photographer can be allowed to disappear even among the knowledgeable because the routines for making such photographs and their fidelity to the original are taken for granted, most importantly assumed to have no influence on the material photographed. This mechanical reproduction which seems unmediated suggests a kind of *stand-for* relation which is in some sense pure. The photograph stands for the object it represents without human intervention or interpretation.

Semiosis without Authors

There is nothing unfamiliar about semiosis without authors though we generally refer to it in a rather different way; we think of it as the cause/effect relation. When we refer to such things as clouds being a sign of rain or smoke being a sign of fire we are still involved in an act of semiosis but we have eliminated the mediating author. The emergence of science as an important element in our lives has elevated this special kind of semiosis to a position of importance which makes it seem as though it is a different kind of phenomenon; but the difference is one of degree not kind — the scientific way of thinking differs only in the degree of certainty it attaches to its reading of 'texts'. The 'texts' which scientists read are the various domains defined by their reading instruments.

The transition from a rule of understanding to a law of nature seems to be an abrupt shift from the mutable to the immutable; but the many shades of uncertainty even in the most developed of the physical sciences actually make this shift gradual rather than abrupt. The shift always occurs at the point where the projected author is abandoned. We have seen this happen when a text is read as a product of a culture and when a scientist assumes no mediating or guiding influence on the 'texts' he studies.

Change and Regularity

Some readers may be disturbed at the lack of any fixed way of understanding photographs or, by implication, any other text, and may be alarmed at my suggestion that science is just another kind of reading. It may seem that I am offering a recipe for anarchy with no fixed point from which to proceed, and suggesting that we can read the world as we choose, that there are no truths, only the constant shifting of positions. This is not so. The analysis I have given of reading could not have been developed without a clear sense of the regularities in reading. We cannot determine the nature of any particular text — truth is not to be found at that level which is constantly subject to change owing to different readings and readings of readings. But when we examine the process of reading itself, we find a clear sense of regularity and order which enables us to account for the changes at the level of the text itself.

We can return to the metaphor of the landscape which I invoked earlier. Asking for the text itself to display a regularity is like asking of a landscape that it appear the same no matter what position one looks at it from. Because we are so used to the changing appearance of the world as we move about it, we notice a different level of regularity and order. Thus my exegesis on the reading of texts should not be seen as an abandonment of all desire for order or understanding; on the contrary, it is a search for a better order of understanding.

Summary

Another step in unpacking the reading process is to understand the elimination of projected authors. In the first instance the elimination of projected authors enables the critic or scholar to exercise a spurious authority over the text. Secondly, there are many processes of transcription or reproduction where it has become conventional to ignore the chain of authors that occupy the space between the reader and some original text. Finally, the elimination of authorship is at the boundary between the semiotics of communication and the remainder of the vast semiotic domain.

THE PROBLEM OF MEANING

Give me a firm spot on which to stand, and I will move the earth.
(Archimedes)

Introduction

Nowhere in semiotics is the sense of uncertainty more obvious and profound than in relation to meaning. If there is any single idea in semiotics which threatens the entire enterprise it is meaning. Meaning is the pivot in semiotics, the point of leverage in the life of signs. The meaning of a sign tells us about its place in the world: its origin and how we might use it. 'Sign' and 'meaning' are inextricable; to identify something as a sign is in the next breath to interrogate its meaning, for it is in the nature of signs (or so it would seem) to have meaning.

Much of the recent history of semiotics is woven into a political debate about the nature and influence of the meanings, either implicit or explicit, in mass communication. In Britain this became manifest in Communication and Cultural Studies, which grew out of the seminal works of Raymond Williams and Richard Hoggart and which turned, in the early 1970s, to French structuralist and post-structuralist semiotics for analytic tools and methods of inquiry. These methods promised initially, but failed to deliver, a science of meaning that would enable its users to analyse the most recondite levels of meaning conveyed by mass media messages. This was not to be a simple account, a catalogue of message meanings, but an analysis of the way in which meaning was formed by the structure of messages, the hidden ideology of the state and the deepest processes of the unconscious mind. A powerful brew of ideas was concocted and its heady vapours have led many to hallucinate a sense of dominion over meaning. At times this tradition has displayed a gargantuan and self-destructive obsession with theory; everything has to be 'theorised' (to use one of the many tortured neologisms it has given rise to). Whatever other issues have been debated within this tradition, and there are many important matters that came bubbling up in this rich soup, the most important has been the meanings of messages. All the analytical tools and conceptual engines of this vague and sometimes obscure system of thought converge on meaning.

Considering meaning's central position it is therefore surprising to find the following entry in a recent summary of key concepts in the area.

> **meaning** * The import of any signification * Meaning is a largely untheorized term, although debates about the meaning of meaning are well-known conversation stoppers. In the context of communication studies, it is worth bearing in mind that meaning is the object of study, not a given or self-evident quantum that exists prior to analysis. Hence meaning should not be assumed to reside *in* anything, be it text, utterance, programme, activity or behaviour, even though such acts and objects may be understood as meaningful. Meaning is the product or result of communication, so you will doubtless come across it frequently. But don't expect conceptual precision from it, and whenever you find it, pluralize it. (O'Sullivan *et al.* 1983, p. 132)

This casual, almost dismissive entry belies a deeper uncertainty and failure. In the first place it is not true that meaning is 'untheorized'. For anyone who is interested there is a substantial theoretical literature on the subject within the philosophy of language. Indeed it would be reasonable to suggest that meaning was *the* theoretical issue in the philosophy of language. The absence of any sustained engagement with issues in the philosophy of language points to a serious intellectual hermeticism within the tradition of British Communication Studies. Secondly, if the central object of study is quite so poorly conceptualised, what value can one attach to any so-called conclusions or findings about meaning? Before it has even been 'theorised' into existence it is 'pluralised' out of significance.

The rest of this entry, namely that meaning is a product of communication, hints at the essential difficulty of studying meaning; it is towards understanding that difficulty that this chapter is devoted.

Meaning as Product

One of the discoveries made by philosophers, in their attempts to cut through the tangle of ordinary language and arrive at a clearing of conceptual clarity and truth, is that words are multipurpose tools that can be used on different occasions to perform quite different tasks; and it is very easy to slip and slide between these different usages unless one applies rigorous standards of argument. It may well be that this is not really a philosophical discovery but in fact a sensitive observation on the ethnography of natural languages. As one might expect, the word 'meaning' has many different uses, but because it is not only a word *in* the language but also a word *about* language, it causes special problems. The meaning of meaning is not just a 'well-known conversation stopper'; thought and study about the nature of language or any other kind of semiotic phenomenon are seriously undermined without some clear definition.

From the earlier chapters of this book there has emerged a principle of study in semiotics. Whether we are studying an entire text or a single word such as 'meaning', it is always necessary to ask, '*where am I in relation to the thing studied?*'. Any observation about the use of a word has other uses conflated within it, in the form of authors or readers, so that when philosophers pluck sentences out of usage or invent improbable statements to test usage they are not working in an abstract realm purely concerned with formal analysis. Linguistic philosophers are like puppeteers whose strings are the projected authors and readers. The strings move like shadows just out of sight, supporting and animating the words. The trick, as with real puppetry, is to make it seem as though the puppets — in this case the words — have a life of their own. This is the stuff out of which abstract philosophical analysis is formed.

It is Wittgenstein, in *Philosophical Investigations*, a book which is quite openly and explicitly populated by projected readers and authors, who most clearly argues that meaning should be understood in terms of usage and this seems eminently sensible and straightforward (Wittgenstein 1953). Language, in this view, is part of the human ability to make and use tools. But we need to extend this metaphor of the tool a little further and ask how this tool works; what is its principal mode of operation? It is at this point that most philosophy deserts us. Wittgenstein performed an elegant and often enigmatic dance around this question but never confronted it. Language is what we call our sense of the conglomerate of instances in which signs and referents come together; but how is this achieved? What is the pivot and lever of this process that allows signs, such as words, and things to come together? Wittgenstein in the end falls back on the primitive notion of communication as sharing and we have already seen the circularity of this idea. It does not explain how sign and referent come together. It simply asserts the public nature of the conglomerate.

In order to break the circle and the silence two additions need to be made to this idea. First, language works not through some unspecified contact or sharing but through semiosis: the *stand-for* relation. *Sign and referent are brought together by the process of semiosis*. Second, each use of the language whether in a complex text or in the analysis of a single word such as 'meaning', involves a fresh instance of semiosis. Because the word 'meaning' is both in and about language, then each time we use it, each time we ask what it stands for, our answer ripples through all of what we understand by 'language'. It is impossible to enter the pool of language, as it were, without disturbing the water.

Meaning is thus the end product of the application of a special kind of tool — semiosis. In semiotics, therefore, we face a unique problem. If we try to study meaning we are studying what we ourselves produce.

Quantum Theory and Semiotics

The meaning of a sign at any moment can be a shimmering mirage that refracts, changes and takes on a new form as we approach it. This disturbing state of affairs is not without precedent. Meaning is like the capricious sub-atomic particles of quantum mechanics which defy the observer's ingenuity; traces of its presence are all around us but attempts to observe it change it irreversibly into a new form, no more stable than its parent. Within the peculiar world of quantum mechanics we find something similar to the problem of meaning in semiotic research.

Before proceeding to spell out the implication of this view for the study of semiotics, it is worth considering how physicists have tried to come to terms with the counter-intuitive world of quantum mechanics. Here is one physicist's view:

May the universe in some strange sense be 'brought into being' by the participation of those who participate? . . . The vital act is the act of participation. 'Participator' is the incontrovertible new concept given by quantum mechanics. It strikes down the term 'observer' of classical theory, the man who stands safely behind the thick glass wall and watches what goes on without taking part. It [i.e. observing] cannot be done, quantum mechanics says. (Wheeler *et al.* 1973, p. 1273)

It would seem that physicists have come to terms with their removal from 'behind the thick glass wall' but the old habits of mind die hard. What has in fact happened is the establishment of an uneasy truce between the old 'observer' and the new findings without a radical transformation to 'participation'. The logic of classical ideas about the nature of knowledge which separates the knower from the known is too much part of the fabric of scientific thinking to be overturned by the radical findings of quantum theory.

These findings are frequently represented by using mathematical diagrams known after their inventor as Feynman diagrams. They are the physicist's equivalent of the diagrams of the communication

Figure 8.1: Feynman Diagram

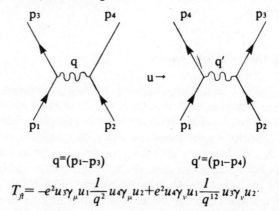

$$q=(p_1-p_3) \qquad\qquad q'=(p_1-p_4)$$

$$T_{fi}= -e^2 u_3\gamma_\mu u_1 \frac{1}{q^2} u_4\gamma_\mu u_2 + e^2 u_4\gamma_\nu u_1 \frac{1}{q'^{12}} u_3\gamma_\nu u_2.$$

process with which I began Chapter 2. They provide a model of the world as viewed by an outsider; they do not include the observer. The only concession that Feynman diagrams make to quantum theory's 'participant' is to allow for different diagrams being drawn to represent the same phenomenon, depending on the kind of observation that is made. This allows the old idea of the observer to persist but in a modified form which says 'This is what you will bserve if you look in this way, but if you change your way of ooking you will observe the world in a different way'. All that lters in this modified scheme is the way of looking. The scientist till observes rather than participates, and the world, though mpossible to understand from a single point of view, remains nchanged. In a way what has happened in physics is that a new rinciple of *observation* has been created. The knower is still eparated from the known but the relation between the two is now luralistic rather than monolithic.

Two points need to be made about this uneasy half-way house. irstly, at the heart of the physicist's problem is the question: how o we represent the world that we are investigating? This is readily ecognisable as a problem of applied semiotics. What model can we se to *stand for* the behaviour of things in the world? Part of the lebate which has followed in the wake of quantum theory has been bout whether any model of the world is possible. This is a semiotic risis because it brings into question the whole process of making ne thing *stand for* another. The physicists who see quantum heory as the end of the road have in effect achieved a new level of umility by acknowledging that there may be limits to the human apacity of semiosis. They are suggesting that there is in principle a imit to the human capacity to generate meaning and under- tanding. This is a fascinating question which is critical to all our nterprises. If I, as a writer, fail to generate an appropriate netaphor, is it because of a failure of imagination or creative skill, r is it because I have come up against the limits of what is semioti- ally possible? From this perspective the limits of understanding in hysics are fundamentally semiotic and the physicist has joined the ovelists and poets in our century who have recognised that the rich exture of life can only be partially represented and dimly grasped n our imaginative constructions.

Secondly, it is clear from Feynman diagrams that there has been a failure within physics to articulate a logic of positions which would be a necessary part of any fully participatory science. There s no set of diagrams, notation or calculus in physics which is quivalent to the notation developed in this text. In a sense physics has paid lip service to its own discovery. Since quantum theory was ntroduced there has been no diminution of concentration on the 'observations' of matter; in fact there has been an increased emphasis on models that are strategically intended to cleanse obser- vations of the taint of the observer. This is understandable if we see

physics as taking place within the culture of science which fiercel
defends the principle of objectivity. 'Participation' from a positio
of scientific orthodoxy must seem like the heresy of subjectivit
which at all costs must be purged from scientific thinking just as th
honest politician seeks to rid the body politic of graft and corrup
tion. Some physicists have hoped that in the end quantur
mechanics will turn out to be nothing but a bad dream from whicl
physics will wake up into the clear light of scientific understanding
but until that happens, or until physics finds out that it is wid
awake and begins with due humility to articulate its own logic o
positions, semiotics is on its own; it may be that the decisiv
advance in understanding in physics will come from development
and discoveries in semiotics.

There are, however, legitimate reasons why physics has not had
very strong need to develop a logic of positions and why such
development is essential in semiotics. Physics makes accurate pre
dictions about the world. Semiotics makes none. This fundamenta
difference tends to be glossed over by those who seek to elevat
semiotics to the status of a science, like Umberto Eco, for example
who has drawn attention to the similarities between quantur
physics and semiotics.

> . . . *every time a structure (of meanings) is described somethin*
> *occurs within the universe of signification which no longer make*
> *it completely reliable.*

But this condition of imbalance and apparent lack of stability
puts semiotics on a par with other disciplines such as physics
governed — as this latter is — by such methodological criteria a
the indeterminacy or complementarity principles. Only if i
acquires this *awareness of its own limits*, and avoids aspiring tc
an absolute form of knowledge, will one be able to consider
semiotics a *Scientific discipline.* (Eco 1976b, p. 129, Eco's italics

But Eco misses a critical difference between physics and semiotics. The influence of the observer and the limits of indeterminacy
are accurately predictable in quantum theory. In fact the reaso
why quantum theory has been accepted within physics is because al
its predictions have been confirmed by observations. In semiotics,
however, the indeterminacy is much more profound. We have nc
theory of semiotics which allows us to make any predictions —
even of a statistical kind — about the 'universe of signification'.

Even at the level of a specific semiotic system prediction is elusive. Eco, even in his recent writing, persists in his belief in a scientific semiotics, but has to resort to circular arguments in its defence:

> Being scientific, a specific semiotics can have a *predictive* power: it can tell which expressions, produced according to the rules of a given system of signification, are acceptable or 'grammatical', and which ones a user of the system would presumably produce in a given situation. (Eco 1984a, p. 99, Eco's italics)

All this argument tells us is that if we describe a set of rules we can recognise when someone breaks them and that if someone uses a set of rules they are likely to follow them. Eco mistakes description and prescription for prediction. Semiotics as a science in some sense comparable to physics is either a long way off in the future or, as I shall argue, a misconception of the nature of semiotic inquiry. Because of the very predictability of physical phenomena, physicists have not found it nesessary to develop a logic of positions. Simple categories such as 'here' and 'there' are still at the basis of positionality in physics. The logic of positions in semiotic research, as already developed in this book, involves a much more elaborate system of categories and relations than those in physics. But, as will be apparent, such a system is necessary in semiotics in a way which is quite different from an awareness of the position of the 'observer' in physics.

In the end the analogy with quantum mechanics fails as does any analogy, but the point of failure with this particular analogy marks a critical difference at an empirical level. It may be that at a more abstract level the implications of semiotics and modern physics can come together more productively. There is an underlying sense in which they both bring into question the idea of a detached outsider, but most importantly, in the rhetoric legitimising its area of study, semiotics can point to the fact that there is another and highly respected area of study which gives the researcher a special place in the 'making' of that which is studied. But whereas the physicist might talk about the concept of 'participation', the semiotician has to talk about 'production', because the meaning that semiotics studies is *produced* by the researcher. *The consequence of defining meaning in terms of use is that the researcher is also a user and as his use is in some respects different from anybody else's, so the meaning he produces will be different.*

Figure 8.2: Fragile Symbol

Such a notion may seem difficult to grasp when put in abstract terms but it is readily apparent through an example. The public information symbol in Figure 8.2 is widely used to stand for 'fragile, handle with care'. In a simple and common use of the term 'meaning' we would say that the meaning of the symbol *is* fragile, handle with care. This statement can be unpacked using the logic of positions. Clearly the position I am in is that of a reader, but as we might suspect this is a far from simple relation. Using the symbol as an example in this text is like quoting, that is repeating what somebody else said at a different time and in a different place. This brings about a subtle but noticeable change in meaning — an effect of a shift in positions which, though common, is quite complex; by putting the symbol in this book and giving its meaning, I am inferring or assuming something about its authorship and reading elsewhere — quite obviously I have not put it in the book in order to suggest that this book is fragile (though it would be nice if my readers handled it with some mental care). The way we make sense of it at this remove is by imagining it having been placed by someone (a projected author) on some object in transit, being read by someone whose job is to handle the object in transit (a projected reader of my projected author). This set of relations is packed into the seemingly simple statement about the meaning of the symbol. In other words the statement about meaning is a story about the reading of the symbol. It tells us what might have happened.

From what is known about people's ability to understand such symbols there is a strong possibility that its 'meaning' will be 'misunderstood'. Or, to put the matter more neutrally, the meaning produced by an actual reader may not be the same as the meaning given by the projected reader of my projected author. I have created a convenient fiction about the reading of this symbol. The meaning of the symbol has compressed within it a story about its use elsewhere. At the beginning of this paragraph I gave the meaning in unequivocal terms. It is not difficult to see how the meaning I have thereby produced is different from the meaning that might arise say in a foreign port where an illiterate itinerant dock worker may have had the job of unloading the cargo on which the symbol was placed. We can never isolate meaning from its context of usage. Even the attempt to do so ends up in creating a new context which in some way creates a new meaning. This points to a most interesting feature which will be developed further in a later chapter; semiosis is potentially a creative activity.

Are Meanings in Objects?

At this point some philosophers might be inclined to put forward the counter-argument that the meaning of the symbol is not dependent on any actual or possible outcome but is an intrinsic property of the symbol, that the meaning is not a product of creative imagination but a property of the object. The meaning of the symbol, they would argue, is not dependent on its interpretation. They might wish to generalise the argument even further and suggest that signs have meanings independent of any user, suggesting, for example, that the plaque on the Pioneer space craft, which carries messages about us and our planet beyond the solar system, will still have its meaning even if no being ever finds it and if it survives after the last human disappears from the universe.

The trouble with this argument is that it involves an intellectual sleight of hand, though a very elegant one. The argument asks us to conduct a kind of thought experiment: to imagine the existence of a sign in a context where there is no one to read it. Such a position is easily imagined, but the next part involves the trick; the only way to conduct our thought experiment is to read the sign, in its unusual context, and see whether it retains its meaning. In other words we must imagine ourselves *reading* a sign in a place where there are no

readers! We cannot simply look at the sign; as I have pointed ou
already, simply to recognise something as a sign is to become a
reader. We can well imagine a place where there are no readers bu
when we visit that place, even in our imaginings, we go as readers
We can therefore never test the philosopher's argument. It is like
asking someone to imagine what it is like to breathe in a vacuum or
float in an empty pool.

The philosophy of language is littered with such thought experiments which ask us to detach ourselves from language in use and
pretend it exists in a neutral zone. The usual method involves
taking a sentence and pretending that it can exist and have a
meaning or a clear grammatical structure independently of any
reader. This pretence is sometimes maintained by stating that
linguistic philosophers observe while everyone else reads, and is
shattered by pointing out that reading a text in linguistic
philosophy is, when all is said and done, still reading. A more
sophisticated but equally flawed method is to claim that the
philosopher or reader of the philosophical text *shares* the same
linguistic competence as other members of the same linguistic community. I have already explored the logic of that claim and showed
some of its pitfalls.

Meaning and Scholarship

Arguments that meanings are intrinsic properties of objects do not
only come from philosophers. There are many traditions of
scholarship which are founded on the premise that the objects they
study have some intrinsic value which is either wholly or partly
related to their meaning; this is the case, for example, in some
forms of biblical exegesis, literary studies or art history. Not sur-
prisingly, scholars in these fields have advanced many arguments to
counter the idea that meaning is as seemingly ephemeral as I
suggest and these arguments cannot be brushed aside lightly. After
all, it seems intuitively to be the case that the works of Shakespeare,
say, have an intrinsic quality which is not dependent on any particular reader; or that a painting of a vase of flowers by Van Gogh
cannot be made to mean anything a reader chooses it to mean.

All of the arguments offered, however plausible, are reducible to
assertions about authors or readers. They can be more or less
general, but whichever form the argument takes, some aspect of

either the authorship or the reading of the work is taken to be invariant and as a consequence meaning is in some degree stabilised. Here are some of those arguments in generalised form.

1. The text is the expression of an *author's* intention therefore the meaning cannot change.

2. A text is an expression of the *culture* in which it was produced therefore the meaning cannot change.

3. The text is about eternal truths which are applicable to *all people at all times*, therefore the meaning does not change.

4. The text is structured in a code or language which *all members of a particular society share*, therefore the meaning is constant within that society.

5. *I* understand the meaning of this text and, as *everybody else is the same as me*, the meaning is constant.

6. *I* am an authority on the meaning of this text, therefore it should be *read* as *I* prescribe and hence the meaning is constant.

The methods which have been developed in this text can be used to expose the form any particular argument about meaning might take. However, the reader should realise that the ways in which these arguments are couched are seldom as easily recognisable as I have presented them here; they frequently have to be ferreted out from the interstices of critical writing. But whether they are clearly visible or hidden like the puppeteer's strings, they are always there. They all suggest that meaning has already been formed and therefore the present reader can only reproduce what is available in or through the text.

All these arguments try to narrow down the range of alternatives open to the reader. As such they are attempts to control the reader's freedom. Readers do not have total freedom. No social oragisation is possible without some prescription and nowhere is this more obviously so than in relation to human communication. The methods in this book are aids to questioning authority and to subverting power, particularly when that power is being exercised in someone else's interest, conflicting with one's own. In an information-based society, freedom of meaning may well be the greatest and most important freedom of all.

Summary

Meaning is central to semiotics and an important theoretical issue in the philosophy of language. Language is itself a conglomerate of signs and referents used by a particular community. Meaning is a product of the process of semiosis and therefore studying meaning entails a paradox in which language is used to define the meaning that language use gives rise to. Semiotics shares the problem of position with quantum mechanics but whereas quantum mechanics leads to definite predictions, semiotics leads to none. Disputes about meaning are in the end disagreements about readers and authors.

'When *I* use a word,' Humpty Dumpty said, in rather a scornful tone, 'it means just what I choose it to mean — neither more nor less.'

'The question is,' said Alice, 'whether you *can* make words mean so many different things.'

'The question is,' said Humpty Dumpty, 'which is to be master — that's all.'

(Lewis Carroll, *Alice Through the Looking-Glass*)

Introduction

It should be very clear by now that there is an intimate relation between an interest in social control and control of meaning. There are numerous forms this control might take. In the last chapter I gave an outline of the major arguments which are advanced by scholars to secure our complicity. If we can articulate these arguments and expose their weaknesses then we are in a strong position to question them and, if need be, reject the meanings that are offered. But there remain many ways in which our relations to texts might be controlled and the freedom claimed by Humpty Dumpty might not be easily had for the asking.

A variety of arguments have been advanced that question the freedom with which we can generate meanings. The *stand-for* relation which is at the heart of semiotics may well be restrained so that the production of meaning is guided by vested interest.

Relativity or Relativism?

In an appendix to *Nineteen Eighty-Four*, George Orwell spells out the rationale behind 'Newspeak', a revised form of English from which certain meanings were being systematically removed to prevent thoughts arising which might conflict with the State's ideology. He writes:

The purpose of Newspeak was not only to provide a medium of expression for the world-view and mental habits proper to the devotees of Ingsoc, but to make all other modes of thought impossible. It was intended that when Newspeak had been adopted once and for all and Oldspeak forgotten, a heretical thought — that is, a thought divergent from the principles of Ingsoc — should be literally unthinkable, at least so far as thought is dependent on words. Its vocabulary was so constructed as to give exact and often subtle expression to every meaning that a Party member could properly wish to express, while excluding all other meanings and also the possibility of arriving at them by indirect methods.

There is a long tradition of thought which has been based on the idea that language and reality are closely intertwined. In its strongest form this hypothesis asserts that reality is determined by language; we understand the world through the language we learn. We notice what we have names for and we can only think in terms of the grammar of that particular language. So, for example, if a language does not contain a past or future tense but merely distinguishes between now and not-now, then according to the hypothesis the users of this language would not perceive a difference between past and future. Such a suggestion was made by Benjamin Lee Whorf — a student of North American Indian languages — and is sometimes called the Whorfian hypothesis. It is also referred to as the language-relativity hypothesis because of its central proposition that our understanding is determined by the particular language we use and that understanding therefore is relative to language.

All the various theories which advance such views are examples of *relativism* and there is a simple logical problem standing in their way. If *all* understanding is relative to the particular language in which it is expressed then the Whorfian hypothesis must itself be relative because it too is expressed via a particular language. A similar form of this particular difficulty is to be found in some kinds of Marxist thinking which assert that all theories are historically determined. This proposition, if true, must also apply to Marxism. Similarly Foucault developed a refined version of the Whorfian hypothesis in which he asserted that subjectivity is a category formed by the various discourses of which we are subjects. What then was the discourse that formed the category 'Foucault'?

The superficial plausibility of these theories is possible because their proponents can take advantage of the fact that most of our forms of scholarship do not require the scholar to account for his or her own *position*. One can only claim that understanding is relative to language, history or discourse if one is outside language, history or discourse when making the pronouncement. But, as the theorists who advance relativism are well aware, none of us can escape from the captivity of these all-embracing phenomena. The theories are attractive precisely because they offer to explain so much within the one intellectual scheme. But one has to have had experience outside the prison house to know what restrictions are imposed on the prisoners. In other words relativism is only possible if one does not question the *position* of the theorist using it. The consequence of theorists ignoring their own position is not just a series of grand blunders but also the persistence of offensive modes of thought which, once exposed, are clearly recognisable as forms of intellectual greediness and imperialism; indulging in them is not only like eating one's own cake and keeping it too but also like wanting to eat and keep everybody else's cake as well. Relativism of this kind is only sustainable in the absence of a *logic of positions*. With a properly developed *logic of positions* it is possible to map out the *position* which a theorist occupies *relative to* the subject matter of the theory. In other words it is possible to ask, 'where am I standing *relative to* the object I am investigating?' Relativity is tenable, relativism is not.

European semiotics adopted Saussure's naive assumption about *sharing*, with the simple consequence that only one reading of any text was considered necessary. The possibility of a reading being determined by the position of any reader *relative* to others never arose. By the time we get to Umberto Eco in the 1960s semiotics had become more cautious but also more ambitious. The caution was expressed through a distinction between normal decoding and what Eco significantly refers to as 'aberrant decoding' (Eco 1965). (The term 'decoding' comes from telecommunications and is applied by Eco in a loose metaphorical way to all kinds of meaning systems. The term lends a spurious impression of precision and scientific validity to some very vague ideas.) The ambition was apparent in the fact that semiotics was now trying to occupy new territories — in this case television. As the prophet Saussure promised in a tone full of imperialist resonances, semiology '. . . has a right to existence, a place staked out in advance' (Saussure 1977, p. 16).

This mixture of caution and ambition allowed Eco to map out four different kinds of 'aberrant readers' or what I would refer to as projected readers. Eco describes these other readers as foreigners, future generations, different intellectual traditions and different cultural traditions. It is difficult to see exactly how these four types differ from each other but, leaving that question aside, and assuming I could apply these projections to my own readings of texts, I could represent the result using my notation as in Figure 9.1.

Figure 9.1

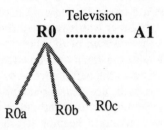

Television

R0 .... **A1**

R0a   R0b   R0c

What is particularly interesting is that all the criteria for placing a particular projection within a category are *relative to my position* as a reader: the categories of foreigner, future generation, different intellectual or cultural tradition *can only be defined in relation to the position I occupy*. So if I accept Eco's method I must presuppose that there is something privileged about the position I occupy. Eco reinforces the sense of privilege by asserting that there is something special about the kind of reading which a semiotician makes of a television programme — a reading which is different from that of other viewers'.

> This research . . . develops out of the belief that what the researcher sees on the video is not what the common viewer sees. (Eco 1965, p. 135)

It is clear from what Eco says that this privileging is achieved because the *common viewer* (whoever that may be) and the *aberrant reader* merely react to the message but the semiotician researches *the objective structure of the message*. By claiming a quasi-scientific status — as an outside observer — Eco and many others who followed him have avoided the problem of their own position within the spectrum of readers. As can be seen in Figure 9.1, all readers are within the domain of the text — none is especially privileged by being outside. There is no special position which Eco can occupy, as he too is a reader within this domain, and the other readers are projections from his position.

There are many ways of categorising projected readers. Plato, for example, in the extract from the *Republic* quoted in Chapter 5, categorised projected readers into adults and children. Roland Barthes offers such categories as 'the French' or 'the public' in his essays in *Mythologies*. Potentially there are as many projected readers as there are ways of discriminating between or categorising people; age, culture, sex, race or class are all possible categories. Any discrimination we can make between ourselves and others can be the basis for constructing a projected reader: 'you' or 'them' are the most personal; the categories used by Eco, such as foreigner, future generation etc. are a possible if problematic way of categorising people. The choice of categories that we use is determined by our deeply-held beliefs about the nature of our fellow human beings. In short, the projected readers we create are consistent with our ideology. Therefore, we might expect the projected readers which are developed by particular semioticians to be a reflection of their ideological position; and this is indeed the case.

Stuart Hall, an important contemporary Marxist thinker, developed a system for categorising different projected readers using familiar, though not indisputable, Marxist categories of class, ideology and consciousness (Hall 1977). The system was orginally suggested by Parkin (Parkin 1972), and consists of three kinds of readers, or more accurately, three sets of rules (meaning systems) that readers can use to understand texts: dominant, subordinate and radical.

The first of these — the dominant meaning system — is consistent with the ideology of the ruling class. It provides a way of reading which accepts the dominant system and is often referred to in the literature as a *preferred reading* — that is supposedly preferred by the ruling class. Using this system of meaning, texts are read uncritically and the status quo is accepted as natural and uncontentious. Notice how this form of reading has superficial similarities with Orwell's 'Newspeak', except that in 'Newspeak' control is exercised directly through the structure and content of language, whereas in Hall's schema control is exercised indirectly by the rules of interpretation which are used in the reading of texts. If this is so then the dominant ideology is potentially more pervasive than

Orwell's 'Ingsoc' but the point at which its influence can be resisted is in the reader rather than in the making of the text. Notice also that the category of *preferred reader* is not simply a description of a type of projected reader but implicitly suggests a projected author; it presumes to know what reading those who guard the status quo would prefer. This involves a convoluted inference which can be clearly exposed using the notation system as in Figure 9.2. The preferred reader can thus be described as a projected reader of a projected author.

Figure 9.2

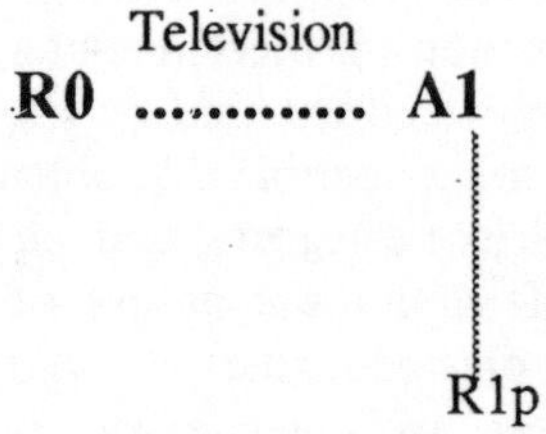

Television

R0 .... **A1**

R1p

Returning to the Marxist system developed by Stuart Hall for categorising different projected readers, the second category of readers — the negotiating readers — accepts the dominant group's definitions of the status quo but reserves the right to negotiate more equitable rights within the existing order.

Finally the radical alternative — the oppositional reading — arises out of the class struggle and, in contrast to the other two systems, is class conscious, expressing the interests of the oppressed working classes.

If one accepts a Marxist analysis of our society then these three categories of readers are exhaustive. They provide a crude general method of categorisation for taking account of all possible readers that could exist within a particular society. Paradoxically when Hall and his students applied this set of categories to the analysis of mass media texts they adopted the false position of the outsider semiotician even though the system uses categories of class and ideology which, according to the Marxist view, none of us can escape or be outside of. The consequences of this double standard were evident in an important study by two of Stuart Hall's students, Charlotte Brunsdon and David Morley (Brunsdon and

Morley 1978). They examined a BBC news magazine programme called 'Nationwide' and claimed that a certain formal structure within the television discourse 'renders the audience rationally impotent' (Brunsdon and Morley 1978, p. 23). This clear projection of another reader raised a question about the position from which Brunsdon and Morley were making their own reading. Had the 'Nationwide' discourse rendered Brunsdon and Morley rationally impotent and, if not, what was the position from which they were reading which gave them such protection? Why were they not struck down with rational impotence? The obvious answer, which seems to me perfectly legitimate though having the consequence of a loss of privilege, is that the position of Brunsdon and Morley is oppositional: they are radically opposed to the preferred and negotiated readings — only they are not constructing a preferred or negotiated reading as outsiders, they are projecting these other readings *from* an oppositional position.

Figure 9.3a

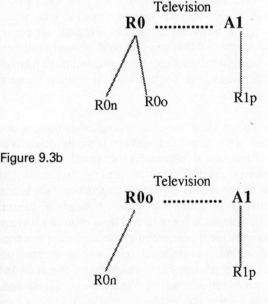

Figure 9.3b

Figure 9.3a shows the relations which characterise the kind of analysis that I could undertake if I followed the above model as proposed by Hall *et al.* The suffixes p, n, and o represent preferred, negotiated and oppositional projected readers respectively. As I have shown, this leaves some ambiguity in my own position, R0. I seem to be an outsider but this is impossible as there can be no outsiders in Hall's system, only three possible types of readers; this ambiguity can only be resolved by identifying R0 with one of the projected categories as in Figure 9.3b.

In a more recent study (Morley 1980), David Morley gives some accounts of reading that seriously question this set of categories but which only indirectly raise doubts about the privileged position of the semiotician.

Dominant Meanings

It is worth returning to Orwell's nightmare and examining the political basis for his fears. European thought has always seen communication and political power as related to each other. My quotation from Plato's *Republic* makes it clear that even in the small-scale society of ancient Greece, messages such as epic poems were believed to exert a powerful influence with political consequences. Orwell's concern and that of other contemporary thinkers draws on Marx's analysis of society. In a much-quoted passage from *The German Ideology*, Marx articulated the relation between class interest and thinking.

> The ideas of the ruling class are, in every age, the ruling ideas: i.e. the class which is the dominant *material* force in society is at the same time its dominant *intellectual* force. The class which has the means of material production at its disposal, has control at the same time over the means of mental production, so that in consequence the ideas of those who lack the means of mental production are, in general, subject to it. The dominant ideas are nothing more than the ideal expression of the dominant material relationships, the dominant material relationships grasped as ideas, and thus of the relationships which make one class the ruling one; they are consequently the ideas of its dominance. (Marx, *The German Ideology*, 1845–6, pp. 35–7)

In one sense Marx was pointing to the obvious. Those in power look after their own interests and they are more likely to encourage vays of thinking that sustain rather than challenge their power. However, Marx offered a sweeping generalisation which may or may not be borne out by evidence. Unfortunately, too much of the ecent work in the Marxist tradition has accepted this generalisation and proceeded merely to demonstrate its truth by ferreting out xamples. It is doubtful that the classic Marxist notion of class or lass consciousness could be applied to contemporary capitalist ocieties but equally no one would seriously challenge the view that apitalism is the dominant economic order of our time; not surprisngly we would expect messages which are supportive of capitalism o enjoy wide currency and support by recognisable capitalist nterests. Nowhere is Marx's vision quite so apparent in our society han in the contemporary practice of advertising. As a critic of Australia's predominantly commercial media system has observed:

The values of advertising are those of capitalism and every time there is an advertisement for a particular product, capitalism gets a free plug as well. (McQueen 1977, p. 33)

But even advertising — the most developed rhetoric of capitalist anguage — is vulnerable in a way which challenges Marx's dictum und Orwell's fearful dream. As we have seen, texts are not autoomous objects. They have an existence which is dependent on heir users. Advertisers, as representatives of capitalist organisaions, may wish to portray their masters as the benign benefactors of society offering us all an ever-increasing range of items to onsume (as long as we carry on consuming). If we accept this proection of capitalism when we read advertisements then we are ndeed, as Marx put it, 'subject to' the dominant ideology. But if ve reject it, putting in its place a self-interested group whose major notive is the maintenance of its own dominance, then our reading of advertisements will change accordingly.

The dominant-ideology thesis, as Marx's view is sometimes abelled, has been at the centre of much of the Cultural Studies vork which I have been using to explore semiotic ideas. Stuart Hall's categories of preferred, negotiated and oppositional eadings are an expression of this thesis. The early work in this line aw itself as offering definitive preferred readings of texts but there vas never any doubt about the political purpose of these 'preferred eadings': it was to expose the mechanisms of coercion at work on *rojected readers* within a fundamentally exploitative capitalist

social system. As Stuart Hall has recently pointed out, the texts o
the mass media are 'sites of ideological struggle'. They are th
battleground on which rages the struggle for hearts and minds. Th
armies and weapons are not the texts themselves but the differen
projections of authors and readers which are the essential structura
ingredients of any reading.

Probably one of the most interesting ideological struggles of ou
time, which has been partially waged on the battleground of adver
tising, is feminism. If Marx's ideas are made gender specific, adver
tising can not only be seen as an instrument of capitalism bu
specifically of male domination. It is perhaps not surprising that a
important part of feminist rhetoric has focused on advertising. I
some respects the struggle for hearts and minds is more easil
waged on the battleground of magazine pages than in the home o
at work. Paradoxically, the most overtly sexist advertising is als
the most fertile recruitment ground for feminism. Images o
blatant sexism, which clearly articulate male dominance, anger an
provoke women to take up the feminist cause. The acts of oppres
sion and discrimination which remain covert and unspoken i
ordinary social life are clearly discernible in the shrill cry of th
publicist. The paradox, which is by no means confined to th
feminist struggle, is that the very instruments which are suppose
to have the power of oppression are appropriated and given ne
meaning; sexist advertising can be held up, like the head of th
vanquished on a pitchfork, for communal vilification. Th
advertiser must appear all powerful and yet defeated at the sam
moment. The great strength of recent feminist writing grows in par
out of a clear recognition of *position*. No feminist can take th
'position' of the patriarchical imperial or impartial outsider
Feminism is first and foremost, by definition, a recognition o
position from which struggle can be engaged.

The use of texts as a site for ideological struggle has as its objec
the control of meaning. Often those involved from an *oppositiona*
position see the task as wresting the meaning from the dominant o
preferred reading position. However, considering the evidence an
the caution by Raymond Williams about the uses of literacy by dif
ferent groups, it is more likely that many of the texts studied, from
whatever popular form, have been wrested from oblivion. But tha
may not be important except in a narrow scholarly sense becaus
control over meaning is sought for political not didactic or scien
tific purposes. The purpose is to bring about a *change* i

perceptions of reality, not to show how language has structured reality, even though the spectre of a distorted reality is held up as part of the argument. This was the great success of Barthes' *Mythologies* and the promise it held out for the future of semiotics. But Barthes was well aware of the contradiction when he said at the end of the preface to *Mythologies* that our times '. . . may well make sarcasm the condition of truth'. The rhetoric of ideological struggle proclaims a victory over the power of the text which paradoxically could not have been won if the text actually had that power. At the centre of that battle is semiosis because the fight is over what *stands for* what.

Popular Meanings

The struggle for control of meaning takes many forms. One of its most interesting and potentially exciting forms can be glimpsed at work in the role that soap operas play in people's lives. A recent study by Dorthy Hobson of the long-running British soap opera *Crossroads* revealed a strong dispute between the audience and the programme makers over the content of the serial. The dispute arose because the public found out that one of the main characters, Meg Mortimer, was to be 'got rid of'. The *Crossroads* dispute is not unique in the history of broadcasting but it serves to illustrate the general point. As Dorothy Hobson observes:

> Television programmes are made by their creators, producers and performers, but a programme only really exists as a process of communication when it is watched or 'consumed' by the audience. Producers and the audience may differ about the content of a programme but 'ownership' of a programme does not normally become a subject of conflict between the production team or broadcasting institutions and the audience. *Crossroads* during this period became the subject of an argument which appeared to be about the 'rights of possession' between the television company and the audience. There would seem to be something in the nature of a long-running serial like *Crossroads* which causes fans to feel that the programme belongs to them and makes them extremely resentful when television companies and the IBA make changes to the programme with which they do not agree.

In the end the programmers, not the audience, controlled the content, though not without some concession to the audience: Meg Mortimer was sent away rather than killed off.

This incident brings into the open the continual struggle over meaning which is part of our common engagements with texts. As the *Crossroads* incident demonstrates, the struggle is not between equals, but there are none the less spaces where meanings can be negotiated, radicalised and even liberated. Exploiting these spaces presents both challenges and difficulties.

Political Meanings

For a long time now political campaign managers and researchers (Katz 1972) have understood that the struggle for meaning with the majority of the electorate has been fought and won (or lost) long before the election campaign. Most of us have made up our minds which party we support before the campaign begins and we read the campaign merely as a reinforcement of our hopes and fears. All the energy of campaigns is directed towards the tiny fraction of undecided voters. The majority, in a campaign, are merely the spectators of a struggle by the powerful for the few. With elections being decided on small percentage differences, a minority are in a commanding position. Much of the apparent power and energy of campaigns is in fact an illusion but it need only convince a small number in order to have the desired effect. Sometimes it works.

There is a subtle displacement which maintains the illusion in place. Communication is generally believed to be powerful, especially through the mass media. We ignore the fact of our own experience — that very few of us are persuaded by campaigns — and project an audience 'out there' which is persuaded. It is the audience 'out there' on which the campaign exerts its influence. The scale of our society allows us (in fact demands of us) that we construct an image of all the other people whom we don't know. The media's power is exerted on our projection of these strangers. We are, therefore, accomplices in perpetuating the illusion of power.

Radical criticism of the media has taken this illusive power as a reality, while demonstrating how vulnerable the media are to appropriation for radical purposes. Unfortunately, the 'reality' of the text has been given greater significance than the 'reality' of reading. In such studies as the Glasgow University Media Group's *Bad News* and *More Bad News*, which deal with the coverage of industrial news, television has been assumed to exert a power over the reader. This has disguised the real political importance and weakened the impact of the *Bad News* studies leaving them at the mercy of the predatory insticts of liberal scholarship. As works of scholarship they are attempts, using the analytical tools of semiotics, to conduct a detailed and systematic post-mortem on texts which have already been consumed. They are littered with references to projected authors and readers despite the stated emphasis on text and anyone who takes exception to these projections is immediately alienated from the arguments. But the real strength and importance of this work is that it provides *new ways of reading*. It is less a work of archaeology and more a work of art. It gives us new ways of understanding the world of texts that surround us.

Fixing Meanings

Much stands in the way of developing new ways of reading texts. Meanings are carefully guarded in a host of ways that we only dimly realise. Liberating meaning from the illusive clutches of the text and giving it to the reader is an awesome task. Yet it may well be that, in an information society, the struggle for power over meanings will intensify. The ways in which meanings are fixed within any society become especially important when a large part of the environment is suffused with texts. As Orwell clearly envisioned, the infrastructure of understanding is not just a social resource but an instrument of social control.

The presence of a system of rules for generating meaning does not of itself explain how these rules become stable or resist change. As I showed in the last chapter, meanings are created in use. They are a product of action rather than the basis of action, so how then do they seem to be stable and independent of particular users? The process by which this occurs is similar to the process which transforms objects into texts by projecting authors or readers onto them. Look at any word on this page and there is a definite sense that the meaning is *in the word* not in your reading of it. Even the way we talk about meanings carries this sense. For example, when we ask questions about specific meanings or attribute meaning to objects the grammatical forms we use are the same ones that we use for describing the qualities or properties of objects. Using the same grammatical form we ask:

'What is the shape of this object?'
'What is the meaning of this object?'

The implication is that meaning is *also* a property of the object. This way of treating meaning — as if it were a property of objects — is common to most languages. It points to a process of *projection* which enables us to externalise our knowledge and expectations and impose them on the objects around us. In other words we *objectify* meanings. What we ourselves produce seems, even to us, to be independent of us. Why should this be so? The reasons are fundamental to an understanding of the social nature of communication and help to explain why the notion of *sharing* is so powerfully persistent. The objectification of meaning gives the invisible social rules a tangibility they might otherwise lack — a manufactured objectivity — which, when shared, makes them independent of the individual members of society. The independent social reality then in turn provides the framework for the social definition of the individual.

Meanings, by being externalised in this way, become fixed as the common property of the group. But for all their apparent solidity, meanings remain mutable products of use and, as usages change, meanings shift.

Meaning and Vested Interest

Anyone who has taken a course in literature will recognise some of the dynamics by which meaning is struggled over, appropriated, and sometimes controlled. The fight is not so much over the meaning of the text but over how the text should be read. The teacher has a vested interest in particular readings. The student who finds Ian Fleming more enjoyable than Henry James or Shakespeare poses a threat to some teachers which cannot be resolved by appealing to texts *per se*. The student can only be dealt with by altering his or her way of reading. The struggle between teacher and student merely serves to point out the unequal relations and interests which permeate reading. In the last chapter I gave a generalised account of the arguments that are given by scholars and teachers to ensure our complicity but we need to explore the use of these arguments against a background of vested interests, in particular readings which arise from the material social circumstances in which those readings take place. We might, for example, take three readers of a television programme: the programme producer, the academic critic and an ordinary television viewer who switched the set on for some light relief before going to bed. The producer has a vested interest in the meaning of the programme, as does the critic, though each will undoubtedly have different interests. Both could incur some penalty in their professional life if the meanings they produce are found unacceptable; by contrast the ordinary television viewer is unlikely to incur any penalty to his career as a consequence of the meaning he or she produces. Through this oversimplified example it is possible to see some of the issues which affect the struggle for meaning. While the ordinary viewer has a limited interest in the critic's or producer's reading of the television text, both critic and producer are likely to have a strong and vested interest in the ordinary viewer's reading; they are both likely to project an image of this person into their own readings. The ordinary viewer probably cares very little about producers or critics; for him or her the meaning of the text is far more open to negotiation and the projections of authors or other readers which provide the structure for these meanings are far less critical.

The retort which Alice could have given Humpty Dumpty if she had had some intuitive grasp of the logic of positions would have been rather different . . .

'The real question' said Alice defiantly, 'is who wants to be master and why?'

Summary

The relation between the control of meaning and social control is explored. The idea that language shapes our view of reality is explored and found to be a form of relativism — a way of thinking that cannot be sustained if a properly developed logic of positions is used. Semiotics following the ideas of Saussure, Eco and Hall suffers from a neglect of position as a determinant of readings.

The 'dominant ideology' thesis is explored but arguments are advanced to show that the dominant ideology can be subverted by appropriating the meanings of the messages which are supposed to defend it. The struggle over meaning in popular culture is explored. We are all accomplices in the control and fixing of social meanings.

10 AUTHOR POSITIONS

The philosophers have only *interpreted* the world in different ways; the point is to change it.

(Marx, *Thesis on Feuerbach*, 1845)

Introduction

The author occupies a special place in semiotics, not as an object of study — something for a semiotician to read — but as the source of semiotic research quite different to anything discussed so far. Throughout this text I have hinted at the idea that semiotics is unlike other subjects. In the previous chapter I showed that semiotics often has the outward appearance of research — a kind of autopsy of texts — but in fact offers new ways of reading; rather than being simply a scholarly pursuit it is inventive — architecture rather than archaeology, art rather than autopsy. The substance of semiotics, though often presented as potential science or new method of research, is neither.

Science and scholarship are the convenient forms of respectability which cloak a much more active and potentially radical purpose. The attempt, however genuine, to capture meanings must fail and result in the creation of new meanings. Moreover, as I have shown, investigating meaning is always in part an attempt to control meaning, which makes any kind of semiotic research political in the broadest sense, that is, it is always done in somebody's interest. An examination of the position of the author will make this even more apparent.

Authors as Tailors

In the preceding chapters it was easy to explore the conventional view of semiotic research as a sophisticated form of reading and to show that, because any form of reading is bound by the logic of positions, certain limitations are imposed on the reader. It was possible to accomplish this elaborate unfolding of the familiar precisely because it was familiar. Certain aspects of the author's position are also familiar and much has already been said indirectly about authors' positions in the chapters on reading. The landscape of communication places restrictions on the author similar to those imposed on readers by the logic of positions. The author must project a reader as part of the construction of the text.

We might imagine an author as a tailor who fashions a text as a garment for the reader to wear. Because the tailor can never measure the proportions of the reader, the garment is designed to fit a projected reader. The major difference between author and reader is that the author fashions meaning by shaping and creating the text, the reader generates meaning by reshaping and recreating, as it were putting on the text. But the metaphor of the tailor is a reading of the author's position and as such does not explore authorship; in using it I am simply reaffirming the conventional view that the basic tool of semiotic research is *reading*. There is something missing in this view of semiotics and in this chapter I shall begin to probe ideas that take us beyond the familiar.

The unfamiliar needs to be approached by degrees. In the first instance we need to locate the author within the landscape, for while there are similarities between authors and readers, as I have already suggested, there are also important differences. I will however begin with a *reading* of author positions.

It is useful to look at the two main ideas of communication which pre-date the logic of positions in order to get some sense of the different emphases that have been placed on the author's position. Using a *transmission* notion of communication, the role of the author can be seen as active and determining. The author is the *originator* of a text and the shaper of the communication process. He constructs a message which is then directed towards the reader. By contrast, communication as *sharing* gives far less prominence to the author who draws on, or is perhaps even a product of, the shared basis of understanding — using the language, or being used by the language, which is common to author and reader. Using the metaphor of the tailor, the transmission model concentrates on the designing of the cloak, and the sharing model emphasises the material out of which the cloak is constructed, in its extreme form regarding both author and reader as part of the weave of the cloth. In the former the author is important, in the latter the author can only be *read* from the weave of the fabric. But as we have already seen, neither of these answers is satisfactory because each fails to take account of the position from which speaking takes place.

Authors' Projected Readers

All authors, including semioticians, face the same basic conditions: readers must be projected as part of the writing of the text. It is as well to examine what is known about the general abilities of authors to produce accurate projections of their audiences before considering the special case of the semiotician as author.

The training of professional communicators is by and large a training in the making of messages. In the training of journalists, graphic designers, film makers or other communication professionals little if any time is spent on developing skills for understanding the reader. In only a few recently developed fields such as instructional or information design is there some emphasis on readers. The crafts of communication are still taught as they were in the medieval period when societies were small and authoritarian; the emphasis is almost entirely on the skills of text construction. If we all shared the same understanding of the languages we use, this emphasis would present no problems. Even if we didn't, which seems likely, all would be well if professional authors could anticipate how different audiences read texts. It is therefore worth asking how well authors can anticipate their audiences.

I tried to answer this question in a very specific context when I was involved in the training of graphic designers (Sless 1975, 1979). The results of these studies showed that design students were unable to make accurate assessments of readers' understanding. Further, there have been many studies of professional communicators, particularly in the mass media, which have repeatedly shown that authors are institutionally isolated from and ignorant of their audience. A study of the producers in the BBC in 1963 described the working environment of the professional programme maker as a 'world of autistic activity and belief' (Burns 1969, p. 72). Many subsequent studies have confirmed this finding in other institutional contexts.

The success of professional communicators is always difficult to judge because there are so many factors which intervene between the author and reader, particularly in complex industrial societies. But even in those areas of professional communication where audience research is used, as in advertising, it has been estimated that the failure rate of new products in the supposedly sophisticated US market is as high as 90 per cent (Schudson 1981). This is not the place to consider this evidence in detail; it is sufficient to make the general point that authors' projections of readers are no more firmly based than readers' projections of authors, and that an important reason for this uncertainty is the very different *positions* that readers and authors occupy. The landscape of communication displays a disturbing and certainly counter-intuitive parity. In the very place that we look for others we are confronted by our own distorted reflections.

Semioticians as Authors

If semioticians were only readers, we would never know them. They would be as anonymous as the lonely viewers of the late night movies who, friendless, dwell on the fringes of social existence — hermits within the crowd. Our attention is not drawn to semioticians in the first instance by the excellence of their reading: it is their *writing* which we notice. Anyone who wishes to be a semiotician must be an *author* as well as a *reader*. The semiotician is therefore an intermediary; he reads and then writes. From this we can begin to sketch out the appearance of the landscape from the semiotician's position.

The semiotician as author is constrained by the logic of positions and the uncertainty of his or her own projected readers. The tragedy of contemporary semiotics is that so many of its authors have failed to notice how little of their own writing can be shared even though they proclaim obsessively that language is a collective experience.

I began this book by giving a position for the semiotician. 'Semiotics', I wrote, 'occurs whenever we *stand back* from our ways of understanding and communication.' Standing back from the flux of life involves leaving a space and the logic of positions tells us that the space must be filled by a reader — a projected reader; texts can never be observed, they must always be read. When a semiotician *stands back* from texts he uses a very special projected reader which I shall call a *deputy reader*. The attempt by semioticians to adopt what they consider to be a position of scientific objectivity entails a subtle though largely unconscious

manipulation of the logic of positions: in order to distance themselves and adopt the vantage point of the outsider, to stand back
and 'observe' the text, they have to generate a reader to take the
place that they have vacated. This reader is the *deputy*. Traditional
semiotic research involves a series of elaborate intellectual feints in
which the *deputy* plays a vital part.

Any kind of reading is an active process out of which meaning is
generated. Texts are like lumps of clay waiting for a reader to
fashion them and give them a structure. If you simply watch the
clay at a distance nothing happens; it remains an inert mass. What
semioticians do is imagine someone shaping the clay while they
observe the process. For example, when Barthes tells us that 'Ever
since the Coronation, the French had been pining for fresh news
about royal activities, of which they are extremely fond' (Barthes
1972, p. 32), he is not reading the news about royal events himself
but is observing 'the French' in the act of reading — in the process
of shaping their understanding of the news. If Barthes' invocation
'the French' seems to us plausible then their readings of the news
will also seem plausible; the latter is contingent on the former.
Barthes at his most plausible appears to be a detached observer of
the French cultural milieu of the 1950s. He achieves his detachment
by creating a deputy which he then observes shaping the clay of a
text. If however, Barthes' deputy, 'the French', seems implausible
then his whole account becomes of questionable validity and,
instead of his position seeming detached and objective, it appears
highly subjective. We tend to notice other peoples' deputies only
when they conflict with our own. Curiously, if Barthes had given us
his own reading of the news about royalty we would have had no
difficulty in associating the reading with Barthes' subjectivity but
the invocation of a deputy, in the form of 'the French', gives the
illusion of objectivity.

I have given an example from Barthes' *Mythlogies* because
readers of this book will already be familiar with the work from
previous chapters. However, the specificity of my example should
not detract from the generality of the point I am making about the
use of deputies. The invocation of deputies is one of the most
common ways in which scholars turn their own subjective reading
experience into seemingly objective research. Semioticians are not
especially guilty of this inversion. They are simply following in a
well-established tradition of scholarly practice which can be found
at work in many different kinds of writing, from the most abstract

of philosophical treaties to the most humble of textual analyses. However, the use of deputies is not a stylistic weakness — something that good scholars can avoid. *Deputies are a necessary consequence of the logic of positions. They will always come into existence when a reader tries to stand back and observe the process by which meaning is created from a text.* If you want to give an account of moulding clay without actually touching it, so that it is free of your imprint, you must imagine someone in your place — a deputy whom you can observe modeling the clay and comment on. Your account of the process will depend on the deputy you create.

The deputy can be given a variety of forms which may or may not resemble the semiotician who created them. The confusions and problems which result from lack of awareness of the role of deputies have led to some highly imaginative inventions. For example, semioticians studying linguistics believed that they could analyse grammatical (syntactical) structures scientifically and independently of usage. They argued that because they possessed an intuitive knowledge of how the language works — linguistic competence — they could analyse the structure directly by reflection without having to study language in use. Underlying this argument about their own competence was the belief that they were basically the same as other language users and hence they could use their own judgement on behalf of all other users of the language. Unfortunately the basic argument is based on a fallacy. Language is always in use even in the rarified examples which litter the pages of texts dealing with so-called syntactic structures. The deputy which regularly inhabits such texts is a disembodied idealised reader. He is a stripped-down grammatical machine — a shadow of the author — always there to use the language as the author dictates but without the outward manifestations of language use. In this way the illusion is created that language is being studied independently of use. Intellectual experiments are so much purer than actual ones. He can observe himself using the language and generalise his findings to everyone else. Because he is observing himself he can pretend that the language is not actually being used. Unfortunately he is a victim of his own imagination. It seems that there is far greater variation in language use than students of linguistics have imagined, so treating themselves as representative of all other language users may not be a very useful assumption. It is of course the case that many language users within a given speech community share common forms of usage, but unfortunately there are not any generalised principles that will indicate in advance what those common patterns of usage may be or how uniformly they are shared. None the less, *sharing* — the idea of a homogeneous semiotics of communication within any particular society — has been very persuasive in giving semioticians a false sense of power in their own ability to judge the nature of all reader/text relations on the basis of their own experience. Their deputy is an obedient reflection of themselves.

A different but equally self-deluding position is affected by those who regard themselves as somehow superior to the deputy: they believe that certain texts will affect the deputy whilst they themselves remain immune. I have given many examples of this kind. In the public arena, the Festival of Light stands as a prime contemporary example. Such moral crusaders, who wish to save us weak mortals from harmful influence, are faced with a curious paradox: they wish to judge on behalf of all of us but cannot do so without adopting a superior position. As moral watchdogs they must remain uncorrupted by the material they say will harm the rest of us. If this were not the case then we would expect to see a regular turnover of personnel in such organisations as each defender of public morals became successively corrupted by exposure to harmful material and had to be replaced at the moral front by new crusaders. It is interesting how, over the years, the same few defenders manage to remain armed and unharmed by all the slings and arrows of outrageous texts to which the rest of us are supposed to succumb.

Self-appointed rulers of the domain of meaning come from both ends of the political spectrum. The right-wing conservatism of the Festival of Light is in this regard no different to the media critics of the radical Left. Thus when Brunsden and Morley in *Everyday Television: Nationwide* assert that a certain programme structure 'renders the audience rationally impotent' (p. 23) it is clear that they are not telling us about themselves but are giving us an account of a deputy — their imaginary construction of the television audience. In adopting this superior position they are simply following the tradition of middle-class intellectual criticism which has been unable to understand the taste-culture of the working classes as anything other than the acquiescence of victims to dominant ideology.

A more neutral pose, but one which asserts the difference between semiotician and the deputy, is that adopted by ethnographers. It is in the nature of ethnographic work that the researcher begins by acknowledging that his own position is one of ignorance. The ethnographer has to learn to read texts by direct encounter with the community being studied. However, ethnographers, with few exceptions, report on their findings using the conventional rhetoric of science which entails the creation of a deputy. One notable and fascinating exception to this is the work of Jeanne Favret-Saada (Favret-Saada 1980), which displays an acute sense of position. (I recommend this work as a useful empirical sequel to my own largely theoretical work.)

Yet another way in which the semiotician adopts a 'distanced' position is to infer that the author of a text has in mind a particular reader who is not the semiotician. For example, an adult watching children's television can adopt a position of detachment because he assumes the text is being addressed to children. If he subsequently comments on the programme it is from this detached position and the text is animated by his projection of a child. This projection is not so much a deputy as a projected reader of a projected author and we have already seen this attenuated being lurking in the pages of semiotic writing. In many instances it is nothing more than an extension of our ordinary speculations about the texts other people produce and our ideas of their intended readers. We can summarise these arguments using the notation as shown in Figure 10.1, where

Figure 10.1

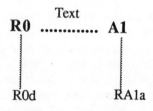

R0 is the position of the semiotician, R0d is the deputy, A1 is the projected author, and RA1a is the projected reader of the projected author.

Thus the practice of semiotics as it has been conventionally defined always involves the creation of a deputy which is then woven into the writing of the semiotician. Even if the semiotician ignores the existence of the deputy, as structuralist semioticians have tried to, the deputy is there, as a careful reading of any structuralist analysis will reveal (Sless 1983a). Thus, as Jonathan Culler has observed:

> To speak of the meaning of the work is to tell a story of reading. (Culler 1983, p. 35)

The only occasion on which the deputy can be dispensed with is when the semiotician shifts attention to the projected author. In that case the text is animated by a different kind of projection but one which still allows the semiotician to affect a position of neutrality.

Thus no matter how a semiotician approaches his material he is positioned in the landscape by the logic of positions prior to and as a necessary condition of becoming an author.

Ironically, the position of the 'observer' always involves the introduction of uncertainty through the singular projection of a deputy or the double projection of a projected reader of a projected author, and this objectivity can only be achieved by drawing on the very subjectivity it seeks to escape. The price of detachment at one level is greater involvement at another. I emphasise this point because it is central to my rejection of conventional notions of scholarly detachment; the subjective judgement of an individual reader is more valuable than the so-called detachment or objectivity of the scholar.

It is important to distinguish between Marxist scholars' straightforward, though politically potent, challenge to liberal humanistic scholarship, and my own more radical and anarchic challenge to scholarly work in general. The Marxists have, properly in my view, challenged the feigned ideological neutrality of liberal scholarship, arguing that ideology is always present: we all speak from positions of interest whether we acknowledge them or not. Liberal scholarship, by pretending to speak from a position above sectional interests, has a false advantage over Marxists who openly declare their sectional interest by offering a critique of the established order. However, liberal scholarship, by its sham aloofness from ideological debates, either tacitly acquiesces to the established order or more insidiously offers a covert defence of established values: either way it is not ideologically neutral and Marxists are correct to shake liberals out of their smug complacency.

My challenge is directed equally at both liberals and Marxist scholars. They both want to speak from a position which privileges their own point of view. They do this by claiming that the methods they use or the vantage point they adopt gives them special access to the truth: an access to some account of the world which is more authentic or real than the experience of the individual reader who is bound by the limits of subjectivity; but the logic of positions demonstrates that in order to do their work they have to be more imaginative than the individual reader, and they actually generate new fictions. Ordinary readers may be content with their own experience; the scholars want to declaim about their own and others' experience. But they have no special access to others' experience: the logic of positions keeps us all firmly in place. Scholars must resort to generating deputy readers and projected authors in order to create the illusion of greater truth. Unfortunately, two fictions do not make a fact.

Many academics may find the inventive character of semiotics unwelcome, something that proper scholarship should eschew in favour of reverence for such scholarly virtues as objectivity and evidence. These scholars will inevitably reject my conclusion at least in part, arguing that, with due attention to methodological rigour and other purifying processes, they can avoid or at worst minimise the joy of creating. However, as long as there is some residual element of invention — however small — and there is no clear method for distinguishing evidence from invention, my conclusion stands. Moreover, it is that residual invention which interests me because it is within that invention that I believe the true nature of semiotics research resides, and all the rest is either sham scholarship or, more charitably, art.

Semiotics as Art

So far my account has not strayed from the now familiar path; my stories about authors are no more optimistic than my stories of readers. But the fact that they are both stories continues to reinforce the familiar ideas that semiotics is a form of reading. I have merely shifted the point of focus, foregrounding the author instead of the reader and telling stories about authors.

Students of texts, whether they come from a semiotic or any other background, share the same position in relation to texts. The hope held out by semioticians that they were creating a science of texts can never be realised. With hindsight we can now look at earlier writers more dispassionately and see that they were in fact inventing accounts of how messages might be read or how they came to be produced. In a certain sense these accounts are fictions, imaginative attempts to describe processes of reading or writing; in some instances they even suggested new ways of reading that undermined or radically challenged more conventional ways. Once it is considered in this light the work of semioticians can be treated quite differently. We are no longer inhibited by the strictures of science but can become more concerned with questions of plausibility and value. Semiotics can be treated as an art form analogous to literature or painting rather than as a science, though it is an art form of a special kind. We ordinarily think of art as offering us representations of different worlds. The world of literature is personal relations; the world of painting is that of appearances; the world of semiotics is texts. If we think of novels as telling us stories about people and their lives, and paintings as offering us accounts of the appearance of things, semiotics can be thought of as offering us stories about the reading or making of texts. And just as with a novel or a film we suspend our disbelief, so with semiotics we adopt appropriate standards of judgement. This does not in any way diminish the importance of conventional semiotics but it does give us a better vantage point from which to judge it.

One of the most valuable tasks that semiotics can undertake, as part of a critical community, is to offer new and challenging ways of reading. It has already done this in many areas. The significant achievement of Barthes was not in the *discovery* of the machinery of meaning but in the *invention* of new ways of reading. The great achievement of structuralism was to provide the necessary conditions under which such invention could flourish and we are all the richer for it despite the intellectual shortcomings of Structuralism and its bogus claims to being a science.

Semiotics thus becomes an instrument of much greater power than was ever anticipated. Far from being the outsider's vantage point, it is deeply involved — enmeshed in the process of life and in changing our ways of understanding.

In its current phase semiotics is a mimetic art: reading mirrors life. The structuralists wanted to assert that texts reflected an underlying reality — the true life of society. In its radical manifestations the argument was refined to suggest that the 'reality' underlying texts was false but served to keep the existing order in place. More recently, through the empirical work of David Morley (Morley 1980) and Dorothy Hobson (Hobson 1982) and the theoretical work of Virginia Nightingale (Nightingale 1984), it has become apparent that single texts can sustain multiple views of reality. However, the relation between reading and reality is seldom taken beyond the simple idea that reading reflects and reinforces particular 'realities'.

I suspect that many people's reading of texts, particularly mass media texts such as television programmes, are more subtle. Attempts at dominance, particularly by the over-inflated and self-important, can be rather easily deflected by treating them as parody. Politicians and news commentators seem to lend themselves so readily to satire and humour, and the world in which they move seems so pressurised and reified, that the very idea that in some way television mirrors reality seems to me a joke. However, I suspect that it is not a joke I share with the impassioned humourless advocates of the dominant ideology thesis. For them the relation between media and reality is a very serious business. They want to argue that in some deep sense the texts of the mass media are read as reflecting a reality even if it is a false reality. However, just as other art forms have developed multiple relations with their subject matter so reading may take on a variety of forms.

The emergence of semiotics as an art form should not surprise us. In the latter part of the twentieth century our world has become suffused with texts in an unprecedented fashion. Not only has our leisure become dominated by texts but a large proportion of the workforce in modern post-industrial societies is in information-related industries spending its working life dealing with texts: in Australia, for example, 8.5 per cent of the workforce was employed in the information sector in 1911, and by 1977 that figure had risen to more than 30 per cent; the USA entered the 1980s with close on 50 per cent of its workforce already engaged in the information sector (Lamberton 1980). Texts have become an important part of life as never before and therefore it is hardly surprising that our art forms should reflect this.

But semiotics' role in creating new ways of reading is only a foretaste of an even more powerful role which will take us one further step into the unthought of and unfamiliar. To take the next step we need to refine our conception of the communication process.

The Elastic Landscape

In Chapter 3 I introduced the metaphor of a landscape which has served us well. Up to this point I have used it to help with defining the conditions necessary to undertake semiotic work as it is conventionally conceived. But in the last two chapters and the preceding section it has become apparent that the landscape is subtly deformed or changed by the presence of those within it. It is as if the contours of the landscape stretch and distend around anyone who walks across it. No matter where the semiotician moves, a new horizon springs up around him, occluding the view, so that he must always speculate about what lies beyond. In this chapter the deformation of the landscape will become even more apparent as we explore further into the realm of semiotics. But this should not be regarded as a descent into chaos; Babel is always ready to overwhelm us but the manner in which it does so and the ways in which we cope with it and hold it at bay are not chaotic. They are subject to underlying regularities and principles. If it were not so then nothing could have been accomplished so far in this text and the strange landscape of communication would not have yielded to any form of mapping.

The landscape of communication is more like the surface of a giant trampoline than terra firma. When a trampoline yields as we walk across it the feeling may be one of uncontrollable and hence chaotic movement but we know that the trampoline is obeying strict physical laws of elasticity which do not change. The regularity is simply at a level which as walkers we have not yet grasped. In shifting from the metaphor of a landscape to that of a giant trampoline I am trying to convey a sense of the level at which order and perhaps truth is to be found in semiotics. Having taken away the security of sharing and the permanence of meaning and replaced them with the concept of relativity of position, it may seem to some of my readers that only the trap of relativism remains — an infinite regress into uncertainty. This is not so.

Some rather wild and woolly thinkers following in the footsteps of the post-structuralist Parisian Jacques Derrida have discovered that they can lurch uncontrollably across the surface of the trampoline, limbs flying in stylistic spasms; and they have concluded as a consequence that all attempts at discovering underlying order must inevitably fail, giving way to the endless play of *stand-for* relations where, like a game, each sign can be made to stand for another sign in an endless chain without ever referring to something which is not a sign. (The idea of endless semiosis was considered long ago by Peirce, one of the founders of semiotics, without succumbing to chaos.)

As Derrida lurches with his drunken self-consuming logic — his acolytes following like whirling dervishes — he fails to notice the obvious: none of his gyrations are possible *without* the *stand-for* relation which, as I shall show in the final chapter, is at the basis of existence. In an ever-changing kaleidoscope of meaning it is the one fixed process. It is the order which enables him to deny order. Without it Derrida could not mount his belated attack on traditional Western metaphysics, which had already collapsed long before under the weight of modern physics (Derrida and his followers seem not to have noticed, and persist in attacking a dead philosophical tradition — trying to shake the soul out of a corpse). The old tradition held on to the belief that underlying everything was some essence, whether material, spiritual or intellectual — some irreducible presence. In denying the metaphysics of presence Derrida has failed to notice his own dependence on a metaphysics of process. Truth is not to be found in things or ideas but in the *process* of apprehending them.

I will have more to say on the subject of metaphysics in Chapter 12, but for the moment I want to make clear that we can bypass the fashionable nihilism which erupted in Paris after the disillusionment with structuralism. The certainty promised by structuralism seemed to exercise a curious seductive power. Like a false lover, structuralism promised love eternal by unlocking the key to a hidden order. When its ardent suitors discovered the deception (which was obvious from the start to many outsiders) they rose up and declared that since their love had failed them — offering no order, hidden or otherwise — they could have no other. Love was dead, order was forever impossible and intellectual suicide the only course of action. Such is life!

Summary

The position of the author in the landscape of communication is explored. Authors create projected readers as part of their construction of a text. However, research shows that authors' notions of readers are often incorrect. Semioticians are also authors and their work involves the creation of deputy readers. The curious demands placed on these deputies are explored. Semiotics is an art form which creates fictions about the reading of texts.

The landscape metaphor of communication is abandoned in favour of a metaphor of a trampoline which enables us to understand truth in a new way.

11

FOUNDERS AND FOLLOWERS

I don't know where he's going,
but when he gets there I'll be glad!
I'm following in father's footsteps,
yes, I'm following the dear old dad!
(Music Hall Song)

Introduction

Now that some of the main elements of my approach to semiotics
are in place it is time to look at the origins of contemporary
semiotics. Traditional semiotic research spans so many interests
and concerns that an adequate history of the subject would have to
include not only those writers who can be seen as directly drawing
on the ideas of the founders but also those who, focusing on
different subjects, take up semiotic concerns: Gombrich's *Art and
Illusion* (Gombrich 1968) must be considered a major contribution
to traditional semiotic research even though the term is never mentioned in the book and Gombrich sees his own work as straddling
the fields of art history and the psychology of perception; Watson
and Crick's work on the genetic code may be said to be semiotic if
for no other reason thån the use of such terms as 'code' and 'information' clearly signal semiotic interests. At any moment in time the
history of semiotics is the reaping of a harvest which has been sown
on the wind, as it were, and has flourished in fields whose
traditional owners may not even have realised they were growing a
semiotic crop. But even the examples given, for all the authority
that they command in their respective fields, are no more than
moments within the semiotic debate. The controversies which have
followed in the wake of these seminal works have focused around
semiotic problems: Gombrich has revitalised an old debate about
the nature of pictures; Watson and Crick have focused researchers'
interest on what genetic material *stands for* and have indirectly
(and perhaps unconsciously) given rise to a more fundamental and
intractable debate about the relevance of semiotic metaphors in
biology (Grey 1981).

Most introductory texts on semiotics begin with the founders, and follow reverentially in their footsteps (e.g. Guiraud 1975; Hawkes 1977; Scholes 1982; Fiske 1982). The intellectual style of these texts is scholastic and dangerously authoritarian with a disturbing absence of critical argument and analysis. My own disaffection with this approach is based on seeing what it has done to teachers and students, replacing inquiry, questioning and doubt with a ritually intoned litany of half-baked ideas which make up the conceptual armoury of semioticians — as if the ideas' validity could be confirmed by constant repetition. In colleges and universities where these intellectual styles reign unchecked, students are given degrees in dogma; they emerge like novices from a seminary convinced of the true faith and are forever doomed to the authority of a single creed for their comfort and support.

With all the authority of an edict, course guides and texts tell students that they will emerge from semiotics able to read the *meanings* behind messages in our *culture* and understand the relations between *texts* and *ideology*. Only after they have been initiated will some more independently-minded students begin to realise that the very terms in which the so-called subject is described — such as *meaning, culture, texts and ideology* — are themselves highly problematic. These terms are the subjects of extended debates. The theories they hold up might collapse at any moment; they are no more substantial than a pack of cards. Not only have students been misled into believing that esoteric jargon is a substitute for understanding but they have had their minds closed to one of the most fascinating and unresolved debates of this century. Traditional semiotics, as I have already suggested, is not so much a subject as a debate about the shape of a possible subject-to-be. There is no subject to teach, only an argument in which one can engage. However, newcomers to the debate using certain texts might be led into believing that semiotics is a substantial subject.

The opening texts of Pierre Guiraud's *Semiology* confidently assert:

Semiology is the science which studies sign systems. . . . Semiology was conceived by F. de Saussure as the science which studies the life of signs in society. . . . At roughly the same time, the American C. S. Peirce also conceived of a general theory of signs which he called *semiotics*. (Guiraud 1975)

The scope of semiotic inquiry is momentarily questioned in this opening chapter, but its right to existence as an independent discipline is never doubted; it is *guaranteed* by the authority of its founder. Robert Scholes in *Semiotics and Interpretation* glosses over the uneasy status of semiotics and says:

> Its founding fathers — Ferdinand de Saussure in Linguistics and Charles S. Peirce in philosophy — were brilliant innovators, each of whom had a powerful streak of eccentricity in his makeup. In his later years Saussure began to find in texts hidden messages — 'anagrams' — that no one else could perceive. Peirce was addicted to opium and to terminology, producing systems of thought beyond the grasp of most other mortals. Yet these two men had truly fertile minds, and the 'semiotic' developed by Peirce, along with the 'semiologie' by Saussure, have led toward a discipline that seems blessed by their creativity, though threatened with their oddity as well. (Scholes 1982, p. x)

Inadvertently, perhaps, both Guiraud and Scholes give us a glimpse of a fundamental contradiction which pervades so much of traditional semiotic analysis: what they advocate and what they do are different things. Semiotics, they argue, can dismiss the author as irrelevant to the analysis of structure but when they want to legitimise the rejection of authors they rely on the *authority* of the founders. Perhaps it is their lack of critical perspective on the part played by projected authors that leaves semioticians so vulnerable to the predations of their own heroes and cult figures.

Terence Hawkes in *Structuralism and Semiotics* is similarly overwhelmed by the authority of the founders as we shall see in a later section. And nowhere is the lack of regard for critical argument and analysis more insidious than in Fiske's *Introduction to Communication Studies*. The ideas of the founders are falsely presented as if they were all contributing to a single corpus — a seamless unity of ideas and method — from which individuals only differed in emphasis. As we shall see, such a view is not only uncritical but it misrepresents deep and important differences.

I realised when I began planning this book that my own thinking had diverged greatly from the founders'; an introduction to them at the beginning would have burdened my readers with a great many difficult concepts which would never be used. This book is not intended as a history of semiotic thought, but in this chapter I want to position my own ideas in relation to the main thinkers who have shaped my work and against whose positions I have found myself reacting.

Ferdinand de Saussure

I have always found it difficult to understand why Saussure should ever have been taken seriously as a founding father of semiotics: his contribution was so slight. Yet a generation of European scholars treated him as the subject's founding father, transforming his tentative suggestions about methods for studying phonetics into a doctrine that was intended to embrace the entire universe of signification. Thankfully, if one looks at other sources beyond the irresponsible rhetoric of introductory texts, he is no longer treated with such veneration, and a more critical and considered assessment of his contribution to semiotics is beginning to prevail.

His main scholarly work was in the area of phonetics and there is no doubt that he made a number of interesting and original suggestions about how research in that area might proceed, though even in this limited domain the problems are clearly apparent.

His most influential work, *The Course in General Linguistics*, is a single volume which, while abstract in parts, is easily readable. The difficulty lies in its intellectual style; vague ideas and shallow arguments are presented with such remarkable confidence that unsophisticated readers of the text might be more inclined to question their own understanding rather than Saussure's explanations. The book was put together posthumously by some of his students from their lecture notes and the style may well be theirs rather than Saussure's. The undeniable fact of Saussure's influence becomes even more surprising when one discovers that he has so little to say about semiotics, or semiology as he called it. The subject is mentioned in only a few paragraphs and what he says is highly tentative. To understand his place in the history of semiotics it is necessary to look at how his ideas have been used.

His concern was to establish linguistics as a scientific discipline in its own right, and he began by making a distinction between language as manifested by the countless number of instances of speech (*parole*), and language as a system of rules which governs these individual instances (*langue*), arguing that the system of rules, being constant, is the proper object of linguistic study. A frequently used analogy for the distinction is the game of chess; in any game there are countless possible moves and at any moment in a particular game there are a variety of options, but the rules of the game remain constant throughout. This analogy is illuminating, giving us some insight into Saussure's ideas, but as we shall see later it reveals some of the major weaknesses of his thought.

Saussure very modestly regarded linguistics as only one part of semiology. His far less modest successors, most notably Roland Barthes, took this idea and turned it on its head, suggesting without any clearly-argued case that language was the basis of all forms of communication, and that Saussure's tentative proposals for a scientific study of language were directly applicable to such diverse phenomena as photographs, fashion, ritual and myth. In the rush to apply this new 'technique' some elementary and important questions remain unanswered.

This is not the place to give a full account of the failings of Saussure's semiology, but readers may find some value in understanding some of the major problems, so that when reading any works coming from this tradition they can appreciate the reasons for its failure, at the same time enjoying the wealth of insight it contains.

The most significant weakness in Saussure's thought lies in his distinction between *langue* and *parole*. At first sight it seems to make sense to dichotomise language in this way just as with a game of chess there is some advantage in separating the rules of the game from any particular game. But the analogy, for all its clarity, is misleading. It is fair to say that the rules of chess are the defining characteristics of the game, and if we want to find out what the rules are, there are many authoritative sources we can go to. From our *position* as users of language the rules of language are not quite so clearly available.

When we learn our first language we do so from direct experience without a rule book in our hand. Most language users are probably unconscious of any set of rules, which is manifestly not the case among chess players. This is not to suggest that there are no rules governing language, but our access to them, because of our *position*, is not as simple nor as straightforward as the chess analogy might suggest; there are many instances where the rules are vague or where a number of different rules could account for the same usage. The only way that grammarians or linguists have discovered or hypothesised about the rules of language is by a careful examination of language in use. In other words (using Saussure's terminology), the only way to study *langue* is by examining *parole*; to study the proper object of linguistics we have to turn our attention to what we are supposed to ignore about language. Put another way (to make the contradiction absolutely clear) we can only study our subject by examining what is not our subject. The absence of any developed logic of *positions* makes such contradictions almost inevitable and leaves the scholar dangerously vulnerable to the charge of arrogance.

This rather simple yet in many ways damning criticism of the fledgling 'science' is not new; in fact, it was through this criticism, made originally in the 1920s, that I first encountered Saussure's name, when I began my own search during the 1960s for semiotics in the Anglo-Saxon tradition.

> [Saussure] begins by inquiring, 'What is the object at once integral and concrete of linguistics?' He does not ask whether it has one, he obeys blindly the primitive impulse to infer from a word some object for which it stands, and sets out determined to find it. . . . De Saussure does not pause at this point to ask himself what he is looking for, or whether there is any reason why there should be such a thing. He proceeds instead in a fashion similar in the beginnings of all sciences and concocts a suitable object — '*la langue*,' the language, as opposed to speech. . . . Such an elaborate construction as '*la langue*' might, no doubt, be arrived at by some Method of Intensive Distraction, . . . but as a guiding principle for a young science it is fantastic. (Ogden and Richards 1923, pp. 4–5)

However, Saussure's notion of semiotics was deeply flawed by the same process of 'construction' in another and possibly more damning way, as the same authors go on to elaborate:

> The same device of inventing verbal entities outside the range of possible investigation proved fatal to the theory of signs which followed. . . . A sign for de Saussure is twofold, made up of a concept (signifié) and an acoustic image (significant), both psychical entities. Without the concept, he says, the acoustic image would not be a sign. The disadvantage of this account is . . . that the process of interpretation is included by definition in the sign! (Ogden and Richards 1923, p. 5)

This criticism goes to the core of the weakness that cripples Saussure's theory.

One can perhaps forgive the French for their customary parochialism in not discovering this criticism until they re-invented it themselves through the obscurantism of Derrida (Derrida 1977). But its neglect by English scholars is less easily explained. There can be little doubt that the above criticism was known. Frank Kermode, in his foreword to the English edition of Guiraud's *Semiology*, says:

> [I]t is a curious historical accident that one of the founders of modern English method, I. A. Richards, was aware of Saussure's contribution, looked in the direction Saussure indicated but took another road. (Guiraud 1975, p. vii)

Kermode neglects to point out that the reason Richards took another road was no accident; it was because he discovered Saussure's road was a cul-de-sac.

Fiske in his *Introduction to Communication Studies* is even more negligent; he misrepresents Ogden and Richards by claiming that they were very close to Saussure in their conception of signs.

> Symbol and reference in Ogden and Richards are similar to signifier and signified in Saussure. (Fiske 1982, p. 46)

Only the shallowest of readings, which takes no account of the explicit criticism made by Ogden and Richards, could lead to this claim. Fiske does not seem to read Saussure very carefully either: at one point he tells us that Saussure defined a sign as 'a physical object with a meaning' (Fiske 1982, p. 47) and immediately afterwards he tells us that the sign is a perception plus a concept. Saussure himself is in no such doubt; the sign for him is 'a two-sided psychological entity' made out of a concept and a sound image (de Saussure 1977, p. 66). However, as Ogden and Richards pointed out, the lack of doubt in Saussure's text is no real help because neither the notion of 'concept' or 'sound image' are themselves very clear or very useful in advancing our understanding. For Fiske, and others who have prematurely championed the idea of semiotics as a subject, such doubts have been ignored.

The enthusiasm with which Saussure was seized upon as the founder of the new 'science' is difficult to understand until one takes account of the protected *position* he offered scholars; in his definition of the sign, there is no trace of the interpreter who is hidden behind the folds of signification. Saussure's attraction did not lie in the plausibility of his arguments but in the imaginative freedom his ideas offered. Ogden and Richards were well aware of the inventive potential of his semiology which they ridicule in their 'Method of Intensive Distraction', but for a later generation less preoccupied by positivism and prediction, Saussure opened up new possibilities for studying material from concealed *positions* which were unavailable in traditional scholarship.

The chess metaphor provides a further clue to Saussure's attraction. The rules of chess enable one to look at a board at any point in a game and plan the next move. In principle one does not have to know what has gone before. The rules (*langue*) are constant and each move (*parole*) is only an expression of the system. Using this analogy Saussure was able to make a distinction between the research of language through time (diachronic) and the research of the system at any point in time (synchronic). Saussure argued that linguistics (and by extension semiology) should emphasise the study of language *synchronicly*. This enabled researchers, using Saussure's authority, to reject traditional scholarship's occasional sensitivity to *position* and freely explore contemporary culture — floating in the freedom of the NOW. But as any moderately experienced chess player knows, the history of a particular game and the consequent assessment of an opponent's skill do make a difference to the choice of the next move. However, Saussure's ideas generated considerable excitement in a generation anxious to overthrow the authority of the past. We can sense the revolutionary mood in one of the most widely-used introductory texts, Terence Hawkes's *Structuralism and Semiotics*. Hawkes's defence of Saussure is characteristic of much of the recent writing in semiotics by being based not on argument but on the scholastic trick of quoting a secondary authority, in this case Fredric Jameson, who supports the primary authority of the founder.

> Saussure's originality was to have insisted on the fact that language as a total system is complete at every moment, no matter what happens to have been altered in it at a moment before. (Jameson 1972, pp. 5–6)

Jameson was one of the early English champions of Structuralism and his pronouncements on Saussure — with such phrases as 'originality', 'insisted', 'total system', 'every moment' and 'no matter what' — do not exactly invite critical inquiry; they are the stuff of manifestos. Buried in such certainty *the fact* about language seems beyond doubt.

Further, as I have suggested, Saussure's 'sign' was just a compound of signifier and signifed; the very idea of an interpreter was superfluous. Radical imagination could maintain its rage from an undetected and undeclared *position* in a structuralist paradise. The absence of any consideration of the interpreter in Saussure's scheme left the space for any particular interpreters to move unnoticed and with great freedom through all the terrain of 'languages', inventing 'systems' as they went. Thus his work provided the intellectual climate and conditions for the imaginative flourishing of new ways of reading, but under the pretense of science or scholarship — invention masquerading as inquiry.

Charles Sanders Peirce

Peirce never concluded or resolved his thoughts on semiotics. His eight volumes of collected works sparkle with insights and display a scholarship which is truly breathtaking in its scope and depth (Peirce 1931–58). The work is like a grand but unfinished cathedral, often with many revisions to an original structure, but with no clear indication as to which design is preferred or how it links up to other unfinished structures. In part this has been attributed to Peirce's peculiar circumstances; he never enjoyed the luxury of being a full-time academic — apart from a five-year period when he taught at Johns Hopkins University — with the consequence that his work is fragmented and incomplete. However, another more profound reason for his unresolved work was his rejection of the European philosopher's approach which was to build grand philosophical systems; he preferred an open-ended view that accepted the possibility that thought and human nature could constantly change and transform. (In this respect he is probably closer to Nietzsche than to any other of his contemporaries.) Thus the huge edifice of his work offers many rich views but no master plan, yet the parts are not easily separable from the whole; one set of ideas may seem independent but in fact relies on others for its support and in turn may support something else.

None the less, the tendency has been to plunder the structure for valuable treasures, fragments of the whole. One such fragment — his threefold division of *stand-for* relations into icons, indexes and symbols — is widely used in studies of communication. Peirce's developed structure was much more elaborate and led to a system of classification that has no less than 66 different kinds of *stand-for* relations, the system itself being contingent on Peirce's complex and original metaphysics. Taken out of context this fragment has spawned a whole library of debate and has provided what seems at first sight a useful basis for classifying different kinds of signs across a wide range of different areas. But researchers keep discovering, often independently and in different domains, that there are serious difficulties in applying the system. Research in text comprehension, for example, is often divided into studies concerned with written material (symbols) and studies concerned with illustrations (icons); but there are many instances where this clear division breaks down and even when it does not it is far from clear what value such classifications have in trying to understand text comprehension, the inevitable consequence of a misapplication of Peirce's system.

As part of his general theory of semiotics Peirce tried to work out a conceptual basis for the varieties of semiosis. He was interested in the problem of classifying the multitude of different kinds of *stand-for* relations. Unfortunately, most of those who have taken up his ideas have seen the question as one of classifying different kinds of signs. The important distinction between classifying *stand-for* relations and classifying signs will become apparent shortly.

Peirce's elaborate conceptual analysis, in which he took such obvious delight, has been taken as a model of the method to be used to advance understanding in semiotics, although the philosophical basis from which others have proceeded has almost invariably ignored the metaphysics in which Peirce's own method was anchored. The problem of classifying different kinds of signs will serve to illustrate what happens when Peirce's thought is plundered for fragments whilst the context in which those fragments belong is ignored.

The method which has been used to assign semiotic phenomena into different categories is a mixture of conceptual analysis and armchair anthropology, mainly taking place in traditional disciplines such as philosophy and aesthetics (e.g. Langer 1942; Goodman 1978), and more recently in Cultural or Communication

Studies (e.g. Fiske 1982). Many taking part do not acknowledge th special philosophical underpinnings of this question. Semiotics is multidisciplinary platform on which many stand without realisin, that they share the stage with others or knowing where the script o the plot comes from.

Peirce and the Classification of Signs

To move forward we need to go back, not to Peirce's comple system but to the way in which he asked questions in order t develop his system. Peirce precipitated a debate about the classi fication of semiotic phenomena. But any classification system mus have at its disposal a *method* of classification. While there has bee a raging debate about which category different phenomena shoul occupy — for example whether pictures should be classed as iconi or symbolic — there is unfortunately, wide agreement on th *method* by which such classification should be decided: in fact mos people who have engaged in the debate are unaware that th question of sign classification does raise special problems o method. Because the questions have arisen largely within aestheti or linguistic debates it has been assumed that the methods of thes disciplines have been adequate to the task of shedding light on th problems involved. This is not so.

The threefold nature of semiosis which I introduced at the begin ning of this book derives from Peirce's definition of a sign a 'something which stands to somebody for something in som respect or capacity' (Peirce 1931–58, 2.228). We can see within thi definition the critical elements of sign, referent and user — th indivisible triad of semiosis. The classification of signs is not matter of classifying a particular set of objects but of classifying triadic process, of which at least one element, the user, constantl changes each time the classification process is undertaken anew This makes the process inherently unstable and resistant to resolu tion, and this instability is further aggravated by the scholarl attempt to be detached from the flux of experience in the interest of so-called objectivity which, as I have pointed out with respect t the analysis of texts, is not only futile but leads to further inventio in the creation of a deputy. Those who have engaged in the classi fication debate have taken the sign, not the text, as their unit o analysis, but the logic of positions imposes the same relentles limitations. Standing back from the sign in order to classify it involves the creation of a deputy, and because each researcher generates a slightly different deputy, each employs slightly different criteria for classifying signs. Moreover, because they all assign different levels of importance to their own deputies, projected authors, and projected readers of the projected authors, they all arrive at different principles of classification — hence the labyrinthian controversy.

To determine the basis for the controversy in this area one need go no further than an analysis of the different projected users that scholars generate. Underlying the debate about signs is a much more substantial debate about the imagined nature of individuals and societies.

The classification of signs using these abstractions, like the classification of museum specimens, is concerned with objects which have been taken out of circulation, and while the classification may be of immense use to the curator it cannot be a basis for re-introducing the specimens back into the world they left. The application of these abstract semiotic processes of classification can be of no practical value.

The classification of signs is not unlike the performance of an autopsy with the wrong question in mind: there is no point in dissecting a larynx in order to discover someone's dialect, nor in cutting open someone's brain in order to find out what political party they supported. One does not have to be a pathologist to understand why.

Unfortunately Peirce himself was inconsistent in his use of the term *sign*. Despite his profound realisation of the triadic nature of semiosis he frequently fell into the common habit of treating signs as objects. Given the way in which our language allows us to treat meaning and signs as objects in their own right, such lapses are hardly surprising. However, Peirce was the first modern thinker to articulate the full scope of semiotics and we owe him a deep intellectual debt because of his breadth of vision. His essential twin achievements were, firstly, to realise that any developed theory of semiotics would be unlike most theories in that it would entail a complete restructuring of our intellectual framework, metaphysics and all; and secondly, to realise that such a framework would have to be open-ended because of the nature of semiosis.

Followers

From Saussure and Peirce there has been a flowering of ideas which it would be impossible to do justice to in such a short book. There are many excellent accounts of the development of semiotic thought and some of these are included in the References. What follows (perhaps appropriately) is no more than a cryptic signpost.

Charles Morris took Peirce's thought and developed it into a semiotics which was consistent with the American intellectual climate of the 1930s and 1940s — namely behaviourism (Morris 1938, 1946). Many of the terms developed by Morris are now widely used (and misused): in particular his distinction between semantics, syntactics and pragmatics are part of the common vocabulary of linguistics and related areas.

The most notable contemporary North American intellectual leadership in the field comes from Thomas Sebeok whose knowledge of the area is truly encyclopaedic: he has brought together many divergent interests including both significant Anglo-Saxon and European work. His view of semiotics is that it is a doctrine rather than a subject or a discipline: a body of ideas and information which do not necessarily cohere into a unified subject but which belong together as a community of interest about what I have called *stand-for relations* (Sebeok 1976a). In adopting this approach he reflects the nature of most Anglo-Saxon semiotics which has been characterised by an eclecticism. Most contemporary followers within this tradition have set themselves limited objectives and avoided facing the more general philosophical issues which any semiotic theory must negotiate.

The European tradition emanating from Saussure has been characterised by the opposite tendencies. There is a long tradition of grand systems in European thought recognisable in philosophers such as Spinoza, Kant, Hegel, Marx and Freud. Thus there is a propensity, even an expectation among thinkers to embark on a grand quest which seeks to encompass semiotics within the widest generalities. Undoubtedly it was this tendency which enabled Barthes to take Saussure's limited ideas about language and generalise them to all meaning systems (Barthes 1968). Within this tradition there have been two major currents. On the one hand there are the cautious systems builders such as Eco, Benveniste and Jakobson and the early Metz. On the other hand there are the radical French iconoclasts such as Foucault, Derrida and Baudrillard (the list is incomplete), whose work has been instrumental in transforming an intellectual backwater into a bizarre cult; simple errors of argument or evidence have been overlooked in order to develop empty though highly mannered ways of stating the obvious or nothing. (Yet ironically, for all its faults, this fashion, though largely ignorant of Peirce, is truer to the spirit of his thought. His view of endless semiosis and his ideas about the power of semiosis to transform humanity all find their echoes and resonance within these fashionable writers.)

While both Saussure and Peirce have shaped the direction of contemporary semiotics, it is probably fair to suggest that the early vogue for Saussure has now been replaced by a more considered reappraisal of Peirce. As more of his enormous output becomes available (much of it remains to be published) his influence will undoubtedly grow. However, the direction he gave to semiotics is not one which I have chosen to follow.

Summary

The ideas of the founders of contemporary semiotics are examined. Introductory texts in semiotics are criticised for their tendency to present controversial ideas without critical discussion. The ideas of Saussure, the main European founder of semiotics, are scrutinised carefully in order to explain why his limited and vague ideas have proved so popular. The more substantial contribution of Peirce is also critically examined. Both founders have generated a wealth of debate but often with only a superficial understanding of the underlying issues.

12

SEMIOTIC RESEARCH

In the beginning was the Word, and the Word was with God, and the Word was God.

(John 1:1)

Introduction

My research for semiotics is nearing its conclusion. By now it will be clear that I see semiotics as a truly radical force in our society. One of its contributions to our intellectual life is in the creation of new ways of reading; this is semiotics in its role as an art. As I suggested in Chapter 10, semiotics has a legitimate role to play in changing the way signs are read — opening up new ways of living through the perfusion of signs.

I now want to develop an argument about what I consider to be the proper role of semiotic research, a role which not only challenges and rejects the conventional view of the relation between semiotician and semiotic phenomena but advocates a new relation. At the heart of my argument is a disagreement with conventional semiotics about the *position* of semioticians in relation to the subject they are studying.

The conventional view, derived from Saussure, is that semioticians study the life of signs within society. Whatever the disagreements which have formed the substance of the semiotic debate, this particular proposition has not been seriously challenged. The objects of semiotic research are given. Semioticians explore the rich universe of signification which is already in place; their task is to understand it. Like other conventional scholars they are custodians of a domain which they must observe. According to this conventional view semioticians do not change signs, they study them. They react to the world, they do not transform it.

However, we have seen that semioticians *do* change signs by the very process of studying them. Their *position* is not as they describe it. The perturbations they create in the life of signs are not the occasional accidental intrusions of an otherwise neutral observer but a natural feature of the process in which they are engaged. One

146

can never study the life of signs, one can only live one's life through them. Semiotic research cannot be reactive in the manner of traditional scholarship; it is inevitably active.

When semiotics attempts to describe the life of signs within society it must inevitably fail, just as a stamp collector would fail if he tried to tell us about the content and destination of a package from an examination of the stamp that was originally attached to the package, but now sits safely in the album. I do not see any future in this kind of research.

Semioticians are never reacting to a universe which is already in place, they are always re-making the universe anew. Genuine semiotic research (as opposed to semiotic stamp collecting) is centrally concerned with changing the signs themselves and bringing new signs into existence. Semiotic research has a very active part to play in the making of our world.

However, the conventional view of semiotics does not lead to this position. Why? The obvious reason is that most of the genuine semiotic research takes place outside the normal range of disciplines and university departments in which conventional (stamp collecting) semiotics is normally practiced. There are, however, other more subtle intellectual reasons, tied to the history of semiotic debates, which are worth considering before going on to our main objective in this chapter.

The Dead Hand of Language

One of the reasons why semiotics has not taken a more active role is its traditional dependence on language as the main metaphor for describing semiotic phenomena. Sometimes the metaphor is applied directly, suggesting that some phenomena, such as painting and cinema, have a language with formal grammatical rules and vocabularies; at other times the metaphor is merely suggestive of some systematised set of signs. However, even when the metaphor is at its weakest, the effect is to give a sense of some pre-established order that is there to be investigated. In its most oppressive form, language is taken to be the root system from which all other semiotic phenomena derive. This was the position taken by Roland Barthes.

Now it is far from certain that in the social life of today there are to be found any extensive systems of signs outside human language. Semiology has so far concerned itself with codes of no more than slight interest, such as the Highway Code; the moment we go on to systems where the sociological significance is more than superficial, we are at once confronted with language. (Barthes 1968, pp. 9–10)

Ironically, Roland Barthes was killed in a road accident. Paradox, which was at the heart of Barthes' thinking, may well provide us with the basis for a 'reading' of his death. Was his death the result of semiotic transgression? Was he cut down because of an infringement of a code of slight interest with only superficial sociological significance? By making language the vehicle for all forms of signification Barthes loaded semiotics into a sign system whose trajectory is steady and slow and he failed to notice the erratic mobility of sign systems which are the product of fast moving semiotic research.

Semiotic Sins

Language is the great lumbering beast, the behemoth of the semiotic bestiary:

> Lo! should a river overflow, he hasteneth not;
> He is secure, though Jordan rush to his mouth.
> (Job 40:23)

In a river of change, language stands firm. There is a parable at work in the use of language as a metaphor for other semiotic systems; what seems at first sight an analogy can be reread as an allegory which instructs us on the sin of pride. Barthes in *Elements of Semiology* provides a commentary on the life of the fabulous beast which leaves no doubt as to the proper *positioning* of the semiotician:

> *Language* [in the Saussurian sense of *langue*] . . . is at the same time a social institution and a system of values. . . . [T]he individual cannot by himself either create or modify it; it is essentially a collective contract which one must accept in its entirety if one wishes to communicate. Moreover, this social product is

autonomous, like a game with its own rules . . . (Barthes 1968, p. 14)

There can be no question of the semiotician changing the system. The mighty beast is immovable.

Barthes does, however, acknowledge that many 'signifying systems' (as he calls them) do change, the change being brought about by

. . . a deciding group . . . [which] can be a highly qualified technocracy (fashion, motor industry); it can also be a more diffuse and anonymous group (the production of standardized furniture, the middle reaches of ready-to-wear). (Barthes 1968, p. 31)

He refers to these deciding groups as involved in a process of 'logo-techniques'. However, just in case these logo-technicians are tempted to imagine that they are actually involved in a process of creating or changing language, he is quick to put them in their place. Individual innovation is an illusion — the individual is merely a cipher within the wider social frame. To consider oneself in any other terms is at the very least to be guilty of the sin of pride. And from the primeval semiotic swamp arises the leviathan of anthropology to assert its dominion over these children of pride.

In a wider sense, we can say that the elaborations of deciding groups, namely the logo-techniques, are themselves only the terms of an ever-widening function, which is the collective field of imagination of the epoch: thus individual innovation is transcended by a sociological determination (for restricted groups), but these sociological determinations refer in turn to a final meaning, which is anthropological. (Barthes 1968, p. 32)

However, final meanings, like final causes, are notoriously elusive.

The highway code will provide us once again with a story of semiotic transgressions: in which a semiotician in search of 'final anthropological meanings' is found guilty of individual innovation. The story begins with the French anthropologist, Lévi-Strauss, whose ideas, like Barthes', derived in part from Saussure. However, his ambitions extended to that supposedly final level of meaning — the anthropological. Lévi-Strauss asserted that our cultures are structured in accordance with principles that derive from the basic structure of the human mind (no less). Everything, he claimed, is patterned in a series of binary oppositions such as raw/cooked, nature/culture, good/evil and so on. Moreover, these binary oppositions and the various transformations they undergo are supposedly revealed in all aspects of culture — languages, rituals, kinship relations, even the highway code.

Edmund Leach, an English anthropologist, championed Lévi-Strauss's ideas and, in an attempt to explain Lévi-Strauss's thought, Leach uses traffic lights as an example. Significantly Leach refers to traffic lights as 'a very simple example' (Leach 1970, p. 21). The essence of his argument is that the spectrum is culturally segmented into the green and red of traffic lights to give the binary opposition of go/stop because, among other reasons, these colours are natural opposites. He further argues that yellow is chromatically midway between red and green, which is why it is used for the intermediate 'get ready to go or stop'. Hence,

[T]he ultimate object of the exercise is to discover how relations which exist in Nature (and are apprehended as such by human brains) are used to generate cultural products which incorporate these same relations. (Leach 1970, p. 26)

Leach's example, for all its supposed simplicity, involves a complex set of assumptions and methods. These cannot be dealt with fully here but the interested reader should examine Leach's reasoning in the light of an article by Frederick Gamst (Gamst 1975). Gamst examines Leach's claim and demonstrates, by using historical evidence of the evolution of traffic signals, that the present system evolved out of other traffic devices where neither red nor green were used as opposites. The choice of the present colours was based on practical and technical constraints, not on meaning. Further, Gamst shows that when an intermediate colour was added to existing binary systems it was not yellow. And finally Gamst also shows that the spectral qualities of the red and green used in traffic lights are not opposites, nor is the yellow midway between them.

It appears that the 'logo-technicians' from the railway companies and road authorities who developed the signalling system were noble semiotic savages who knew nothing of the imperatives of Lévi-Strauss's structuralist anthropology; they generated a whole range of different devices and colours for signalling, out of which the present red, orange and green system evolved. In other words the supposed 'final anthropological meaning' did not in this instance determine the individual innovations of these semiotic researchers.

However, Leach, on behalf of Lévi-Strauss, does not even consider it necessary to investigate these important actors on the semiotic stage. For him the semiotic universe is transparent. No intermediate authors obscure his view of the final meaning.

> Thus, in investigating the elementary structures of cultural phenomena, we are also making discoveries about the nature of Man — facts which are true of you and me as well as of the naked savages of Central Brazil. (Leach 1970, p. 26)

We might well wonder about Leach's *position* when he makes such grand claims from 'very simple examples'. Is he the humble scholar standing in awe of the 'final anthropological meaning' or is he, as Gamst suggests, indulging in arrogant armchair speculation — a formalism which is the luxury of a scholarly elite (Gamst 1975, p. 289)? Far from being a revelation of a deep structuring process in the human mind, Leach's insights turn out to be the superficial abstractions of an anthropological imagination. He is also incidentally guilty of a rather obvious mistake in assuming that the origin of a form which apprears to us simple, such as traffic lights, can be explained by a simple abstract formula. Happily the world is much richer and more complex than Leach's simple imaginings.

The logic of positions developed in the previous chapters enables us to see very clearly how scholars such as Leach, in pursuit of 'discoveries about the nature of man', have managed to disregard the only genuine semiotic researchers in their midst — the logo-technicians. They choose to ignore the real actors offering us instead their own rather pathetic performances as revealed truth.

The anthropological imperative turns out to be nothing more than a modern instance of the sin of pride in which the intellectual falsely asserts his superiority; it imprisons all our thoughts permitting no real innovation yet allows the superior anthropologist free rein of his imagination. All anthropologists are free but everywhere men are in chains!

I have singled out Leach for special mention in this section only because his particular sin is so palpably obvious, and his argument, moreover, allows me to continue using the highway code as an example. However, these examples — Barthes, Leach and the highway code — should not draw attention away from the generality of the argument. Semiotics in many of its contemporary manifestations has had grand ambitions of 'reading' profound truths from humble material. The gaze of contemporary semioticians has been so firmly fixed on the distant horizon that they have ignored what is immediately under their noses.

The real discoveries in semiotics are being made daily by people in many walks of life who struggle with the problems of creating and modifying *stand-for* relations.

Foundations of Semiotic Research

The development of highway codes using elaborate visual signs and rules of conduct is one of many instances of genuine semiotic research undertaken by administrative bodies to develop coherent and rational sign systems for widescale public use. Unlike our language, which is relatively stable over a long period of time and less susceptible to individual influence, the highway code is a system which is in a constant state of change. And as Gamst shows in the case of the traffic lights, its development is a mixture of many complex decisions over a long period of time, during which the system has frequently changed.

The procedures which have been developed to make those decisions — about what should *stand for* what, and how it is to do it — have undergone considerable refinement in recent years; for example, rational and reasonably reliable methods for the development of public information symbols, which are used extensively on European roads, have only been available within the last ten years (Sless and Cairney 1982a). And even in this limited domain there are a great many uncertainties.

The highway code as a semiotic system may be prosaic but that places it precisely within the domain that Cultural Studies has consistently championed; it should command our interest alongside more obvious cultural material such as advertising or television. Barthes found the highway code uninteresting because it did not obviously address itself to the political issues of the day and therefore could not be used as a site of ideological struggle. However, it is difficult to treat the system as sociologically insignificant when its transgression regularly claims more deaths than suicide. (In passing, it was partly the study of suicide by Emile Durkheim which contributed to the foundation of modern sociology; Durkheim's work inspired Saussure's search for methods in linguistics; and this led directly to Barthes' semiology and beyond. Such is serendipity.)

I regard the development of the highway code as an obvious example of true semiotic research. In particular, I have found the development of public information symbols to be fertile ground for the development of a general theory of semiotics, one concerned with the development of new sign systems and the modification of existing systems.

General theory of this kind is quite different from the 'stories about reading' which are the substance of most traditional semiotic theory. The basis of such general theory is rarely to be found in texts on semiotics, though there are some notable exceptions. At the end of *Language and Symbolic Systems*, Yuen Ren Chao introduces 'Ten Requirements for Good Symbols'. The context of his interest is significant.

> Linguists tend to avoid making value judgments about language and regard the description of the facts of language as the proper concern of linguistics. . . . In the case of scientific terminology and other symbolic systems, since they have been more consciously designed for definite purposes, the value aspects of the symbols are usually granted to be legitimate and so one can speak of good and bad symbol systems. One reason that one does not usually speak of an entire language as being good or bad is that it has grown slowly as an intimate, perhaps the most intimate part of a culture, and therefore the best system of symbols for representing that culture. On the other hand, with the change of culture and borrowing of cultural elements the original language is often found to be inadequate and so changes and additions have become necessary, resulting in word borrowings and structural borrowings to answer the new needs. (Chao 1968, p. 210)

He goes on to document certain problems in adapting traditional Japanese and Chinese sign systems to modern usage. Not everyone would agree with him that language is the best system for representing a culture, particularly if the language is structured to support the interests of those in power. But does not the issue of language change encompass, in a microcosm, the full range of issues that have concerned Cultural Studies? The important difference between changing language and Cultural Studies is that the issues in the former are negotiated through actively shaping the language whereas in the latter they are engaged through armchair speculation.

Chao's 'Ten Requirements for Good Symbols' is only a fragment of our scattered knowledge and thought about the development of semiotic systems and a full account would require at least another volume. True semiotic research is at the heart of our constant search for understanding — our struggle after meaning.

If there is a project which lies ahead for future generations of semiotic researchers it is to systematise and organise the methods for and results of generating new *stand-for* relations. We need to understand the processes we can use to create new languages and transform those in use. If we are to deepen and enlarge our understanding of the human condition and the world our arts and sciences need to be constantly revitalised by new means of expression; progress depends on our capacity to create new models, metaphors and analogies, in short new *stand-for* relations. True semiotic research is at the heart of this enterprise.

Some Precedents

My suggestion about the nature of semiotic research is not without precedent in traditional semiotics. Peirce spent the latter years of his life creating a system of signs for the analysis of logical relations. His Existential Graphs, as he called them, were in his view his most important contribution, and this was after a life of astonishingly broad and substantial scholarship (Roberts 1973). Umberto Eco, whose ideas on semiotics have been heavily influential in the contemporary debate, is better known for his fictional work *The Name of The Rose* (English trans. 1983) than for his work on semiotic theory, and undoubtedly the former is an expression and development of the latter. *The Name of The Rose* is a complex system of signs which allows Eco to develop sophisticated insights into contemporary political and social life.

However, the greater part of semiotic research as I have defined it takes place remote from any engagement with semiotic theory. New forms of representation — new *stand-for* relations — are created in virtually every walk of life. Semiosis is a truly ubiquitous phenomenon and we need to understand our engagement with it directly so that we can transform our world to suit our own interests.

Semiotics as Metaphysics

In the final analysis, semiotics is a way of thinking — an intellectual *position* from which to try to understand the universe.

The arguments I have offered in this book are of great generality. Even though I have focused on a corner of the semiotic debate which has impinged on Cultural Studies, the imaginative reader will be able to see how the issues I have dealt with are relevant to a much wider domain. Indeed there is not a single domain of human activity which is untouched by semiotic concerns. Once the semiotic point of view is embraced, one's thinking undergoes a radical shift so that everything becomes visible from this new point of view — even the most fundamental questions take on a fresh aspect from this new *position*.

Arguably the most fundamental kinds of questions we can ask are about the nature of existence. These questions have been asked in a variety of ways, sometimes focusing on definitions of reality, at other times concerned with the principles that lie behind our conception of reality. A truly semiotic approach to these problems, in the tradition of Peirce, begins with the observation that asking questions of any kind, whether about matters of abstract philosophy such as 'what is the nature of meaning?' or about practical matters such as 'where is the nearest toilet?', involves the use of signs. The answers we give to these questions also involve us in using signs. In whatever way we define reality, we will do so using signs. Whatever the principles underlying our conception of reality, we will use signs to express them. Thus a semiotic point of view begins by asserting the primacy of semiosis. In a sense, semiotics remains neutral about particular traditional positions because it is concerned with the substance out of which all philosophy is constructed.

Some philosophers have argued that logic is basic to any kind of reasoning, and since philosophy is, above all else, concerned with reasoning, logic underlies philosophy. This has led them to look for fundamental principles in logic as a basis for our conception of reality. However, logic is not only dependent on signs, it is *inconceivable* without them, by which I mean that we could not even imagine the possibility of logic without signs. Thus the process of making signs — semiosis — is fundamental to logic; semiosis is protological.

However, this may seem a weak argument. If signs were merely a vehicle for expressing ideas then the primacy of semiosis would only be trivially true. The ideas themselves would be far more important. Like people on a train, the ideas are more important than the means by which they travel. We would not want to argue that the existence of the people is dependent on the prior existence — either logical or chronological — of the train. It may therefore seem that the claim on behalf of semiosis is hollow.

But the simile of a train or vehicle is simply another expression of the idea of communication as *transmission*. We can now draw on the extended argument about the nature of communication that has been developed throughout this book in order to understand why the claim for the primacy of semiosis is not trivial. *Communication is not a process of transmission.* The network of relations that link readers and authors to texts are as relevant to philosophical texts as they are to any other. The meaning of such texts are subject to the same constraints as the meanings of any other texts. Hence the argument developed in Chapter 8 about meaning in the absence of readers has relevance here. Just as meaning has no autonomous existence, independent of readers, so ideas have no autonomous existence without signs.

The force of this argument needs to be understood clearly to appreciate its significance. I am not suggesting that the only things in the universe are signs or texts, or that without signs nothing could exist. However, I am arguing that *without signs nothing is conceivable.* Thus semiosis, the process of making signs, sits at the heart of all our enterprises both humble and grand.

We can of course imagine a universe without signs or with only limited signification. Much of modern physical science imagines a universe of limited signification. The moments when alchemy became chemistry and astrology became astronomy were the moments when the universe was stripped of its rich signification in favour of a single signification — that of causality. However, it is one thing to imagine a universe without elaborate signification but quite another to experience it. Even if we were to imagine a universe utterly devoid of signs, the imaginative act necessary to accomplish this would need signs. Our experience is necessarily replete with signification.

The limits to our theories are much more humble than we suppose.

The Genesis of Axioms

Finally we must probe the fabric of existence in search of the nature of semiosis. I shall conduct this final search by examining some of the foundations of mathematics, because the spartan quality of mathematics enables us to see the operation of semiosis relatively uncluttered by other considerations.

Mathematics and logic have often been thought of as the purest expression of our intellectual life. Nowhere is the evidence of semiosis more apparent than in the abstract notations of these disciplines. At times it seems that there is nothing to these activities but the endless play of signs. However, at the foundation of mathematics and logic there is a curious problem: nobody knows where axioms come from. Mathematicians do not usually put the problem in quite this way but that is because they do not see the semiotic significance of the problem.

Axioms are the fundamental propositions — the basic building blocks — of any mathematical system. There is an intimate relationship between propositions and proof in mathematical systems. It used to be thought that eventually it would be possible to prove every one of the propositions in a mathematical system provided the methods of reasoning were consistent throughout. However, in 1931 the mathematician Kurt Gödel, in a famous theorem which takes his name, showed that in any consistent mathematical system there are propositions which cannot be proven from within the system. The theorem is highly specific to abstract mathematical systems and something is lost by translating it into ordinary language; but I would like to draw out some of its semiotic implications.

Gödel's theorem tells us that any mathematical system is always incomplete. There will always be a proposition that can neither be proved true or false by the system itself. Gödel unwittingly discovered the fundamental semiotic nature of mathematical systems.

The relation between a sign and its referent is always open and never resolved. If I take an object — say the watch on my desk —

and use it to *stand for* the British Army, and my spectacles, perhaps to *stand for* the Argentinian Army, I can use them to act out the battle of the Falkland Islands. However, these signs will very soon fail to represent the battle adequately. I can of course use more suitable signs: tin soldiers placed on a plan of the battlefield would be highly appropriate; but there will come a point when even this set of signs will not adequately represent its referent. This is true of any sign system. That is the nature of semiotic processes. The operations performed on any group of signs will not yield the same result as the same operations performed on their referents.

Gödel showed in a highly formal way that when a system is used to *stand for* the rules of that system, there will be at least one formula in the system which cannot be derived from the axioms of the system. He also showed that there is no test that can be applied to a system from inside that system which can demonstrate as true or false all of the proofs of that system.

However, Gödel tells us only what happens, without explaining why. The reasons however are obvious from the method he used. At the heart of Gödel's theorem is a *stand-for* relation. Gödel turned a mathematical system in on itself by making the whole *stand for* the part. It is the *stand-for* relation, which mathematics cannot explain, which enables us to understand why any system will always be incomplete.

Every mathematical system depends on statements which take the general form 'let *x stand for y*'. Once *x* is given its new status the operations performed on it are *as if* it were *y*. This is what Gödel did in his famous theorem. It should be clear from the earlier chapters of this book that the relation between *x* and *y* is semiotic and all the qualifications that have been made about these relations in other contexts are applicable here. From a semiotic point of view incompleteness comes as no surprise. It is unavoidable.

However, 'let *x stand for y*' is not part of any rule inside a mathematical system. It is the method by which the system comes into existence. The axioms of mathematics come from such humble primary propositions. 'Let *x stand for y*', is the simplest expression of the nature of semiosis. The core operation which links the *x* and the *y* is contained in the term 'let'.

Letness

We have arrived at the end of our search and need to identify the simple nature of our discovery with a special term of its own. We need to speak of this basic quality of semiosis in a special way. I shall allow myself the luxury of one neologism — a term that will identify the core of semiosis and allow us to understand its nature; I shall call it *letness*.

Letness is characterised by a fundamental anarchy. It is subject to no logic, no rules of inference, no causal relations or moral imperatives. We may of course attach these things to *letness* retrospectively or even at the time when a new *stand-for* relation is created but there is no necessary requirement for *letness* to be subject to any imperative. Further, *letness* is not reducible to some other state, condition, or explanation. When a mathematician says 'let x stand for y', we cannot reduce this statement down to some more basic construction — untie its logical knots or reveal its inner workings. It stands alone. *Letness* we may take to be the central metaphysical necessity of the semiotic point of view.

Letness as a spiritual quality allows us to define both the scope and limitations of our own freedom of action. It is *letness* which enables us to create ourselves in the image of our gods and yet at the same time remain fragile mortals forever unable to take an Olympian view.

Letness provides a defining characteristic for our basic humanity. As I sit writing this book on a computer I am daily conscious of the difference between my thoughts and the slavish operations of the machine. What test would be acceptable to demonstrate that the machine's intelligence was comparable to our own? The difference is sharply focused by *letness*. The machine cannot perform this basic act of semiotic freedom. I can. The machine can manipulate the substance of signs in the most wonderful ways but it cannot bring a new sign into existence. It may display the superficial characteristics of semiosis by its manipulative power but it cannot invoke a single new sign, nor can it shift its focus from the *position* chosen by its programmers. If we could create machines that would embody *letness* then we will enter a new era. However, if we achieved such a goal, we would also be faced with a machine that was as prone to uncertainty as we are and its visions would be subject to the same logic of positions that holds us in place.

We are therefore a unique and paradoxical blend of restrained freedom. While we reach for heaven we must never forget that our feet cannot leave the ground.

Summary

The traditional relationship between a semiotician and semiotics is challenged. Semiotics has persisted in its traditional role because of a dependence on language as a metaphor for all semiotic phenomena and because semioticians have seen themselves as above other people. This has blinded semioticians to real semiotic research which is the creation of new languages and the change and development of existing languages. Semiosis is the force which both reveals and limits understanding.

REFERENCES

AAAA. 'The Miscomprehension of Televised Communications' (The Educational Foundation of the American Association of Advertising Agencies, New York, 1980)

Adams, Douglas. *The Hitch-Hiker's Guide to the Galaxy* (Pan Books, Sydney, 1979)

Barthes, Roland. *Mythologies* (Editions du Seuil, Paris, 1957). English edition trans. by Annette Lavers (Paladin, St Albans, 1972)

―――― *Elements of Semiology* (Hill and Wang, New York, 1968)

―――― *Image, Music, Text* selected and translated by Stephen Heath (Fontana/ Collins, Glasgow, 1977)

Baudrillard, J. *For a Critique of the Political Economy of the Sign* (Telos Press, St Louis, 1981)

Berger, John. *Ways of Seeing* (British Broadcasting Corporation and Penguin Books, London, 1972)

Berlo, David K. *The Process of Communication* (Rinehart Press, San Francisco, 1960)

Bok, Sissela. *Lying, Moral Choice in Public and Private Life* (Pantheon Books, New York, 1978)

Boorstin, Daniel. *The Image* (Penguin, Harmondsworth, 1962)

Brown, Gillian and Yule, George. *Discourse Analysis* (Cambridge University Press, Cambridge, 1983)

Brunsdon, Charlotte and Morley, David. *Everyday Television: Nationwide* (British Film Institute, London, 1978)

Burgin, Victor. *Thinking Photography* (Macmillan, London, 1982)

Burns, Tom. 'Public Service and Private World', in Paul Halmos (ed.), *The Sociology of Mass-Media Communicators* (University of Keele, Staffordshire, 1969)

Buscombe, E. 'Ideas of Authorship', *Screen*, vol. 14, no. 3, 1973, pp. 75–85

Central Management Library. *Forms under Control* (Management and Personnel Office, London, 1982)

Chao, Yuen Ren. *Language and Symbolic Systems* (Cambridge University Press, Cambridge, 1968)

Cherry, Colin. *On Human Communication* (Massachusetts Institute of Technology Press, Massachusetts, 1972)

Corner, John. 'Codes and Cultural Analysis', *Media, Culture and Society*, vol. 2, 1980, pp. 73–86

Cornford, Francis Macdonald. *Plato's Republic* (Oxford University Press, Oxford, 1941)

Coward, Rosalind and Ellis, John. *Language and Materialism* (Routledge and Kegan Paul, London, 1977)

Culler, Jonathan. *On Deconstruction* (Routledge and Kegan Paul, Melbourne, 1983)

Deely, John. *Introducing Semiotic* (Indiana University Press, Bloomington, 1982)

―――― 'Toward the Origin of Semiotic', in Thomas Sebeok (ed.), *Sight, Sound and Sense* (Indiana University Press, Bloomington, 1978), pp. 1–30

Derrida, Jacques. *Of Grammatology* (Johns Hopkins University Press, Baltimore, 1977)

161

Douglas, Mary. *Natural Symbols* (Penguin, Harmondsworth, 1978)
—— *Rules and Meanings* (Penguin, Harmondsworth, 1983)
Easterby, R. S. and Graydon, I. R. 'Evaluation of Public Information Symbols: ISO 1979/80 Test Series. Part II: Comprehension/recognition Tests', *AP Report*, 100 (University of Aston in Birmingham, January 1981)
Easterby, R. S. and Hakiel, S. R. 'Safety Labelling and Consumer Products: Field Studies of Sign Recognition', *AP Report*, 76 (University of Aston in Birmingham, December 1977)
Easterby, R. S. and Zwaga, H. 'Evaluation of Public Information Symbols, ISO Tests: 1975 Series', *AP Report*, 60 (University of Aston in Birmingham, 1976)
Eco, Umberto. 'Towards a semiotic inquiry into the television message' (1965) Trans. Paolo Splendore. Reprinted in *Working Papers in Cultural Studies*, no. 3 (Birmingham University Centre for Contemporary Cultural Studies, Autumn 1972), pp. 103–21
—— 'Peirce's Notion of Interpretant', *Modern Language Notes*, vol. 91, no. 6, 1976a, pp. 1456–72
—— *A Theory of Semiotics* (Macmillan, London, 1976b)
—— *The Name of the Rose* (Secker & Warburg, 1983)
—— 'On Fish and Buttons: Semiotics and Philosophy of Language', *Semiotics*, vol. 48, nos. 1–2, 1984a, pp. 97–117
—— *Semiotics and the Philosophy of Language* (Macmillan, London, 1984b)
Edgar, Patricia (ed.), *The News in Focus* (Macmillan, South Melbourne, 1980)
Favret-Saada, Jeanne. *Deadly Words: Magic among the Bocage* (Cambridge University Press, Cambridge, 1980)
Feinberg, Richard. 'Schneider's Symbolic Culture Theory: An Appraisal', *Current Anthropology*, vol. 20, no. 3, September 1979, pp. 541–60
Fisch, Max H., 'Peirce's General Theory of Signs', in Thomas Sebeok (ed.), *Sight, Sound and Sense* (Indiana University Press, Bloomington, 1978), pp. 31–70
Fiske, John. *Introduction to Communication Studies* (Methuen, London, 1982)
—— (ed.) *Key Concepts in Communication* (Methuen, London, 1983)
—— and Hartley, John. *Reading Television* (Methuen, London, 1978)
Foucault, Michael. 'What is An Author?' *Screen*, vol. 20, no. 1, Spring 1979, pp. 13–33
Gamst, Frederick C. 'Rethinking Leach's structural analysis of color and instructional categories in traffic control signals', *American Ethnologist*, May 1975, pp. 271–95
Gibson, James J. *The Ecological Approach to Visual Perception* (Houghton Mifflin, Boston, 1979)
Glasgow Media Group. *Bad News* (Routledge & Kegan Paul, London, 1976)
—— *More Bad News* (Routledge & Kegan Paul, London, 1980)
Goffman, Erving. *Frame Analysis: an essay on the organisation of experience* (Harper & Row, New York, 1974)
Gombrich, E. H. *Art and Illusion* (Phaidon Press, London, 1968)
Goodman, Nelson. *Languages of Art* (Bobbs-Merrill, New York, 1968)
Grey, Bennison. Review of *The Eighth Day of Creation* by Horace F. Judson (Simon and Schuster, New York, 1979), in *Ars Semiotica*, vol. IV, no. 1, 1981, pp. 88–96
Guiraud, Pierre. *Semiology* (Routledge and Kegan Paul, London, 1975)
Hall, Stuart. 'Culture, the Media and the "Ideological Effect" ', in James Curran, Gurevitch and Woollacott (eds.) *Mass Communication and Society* (Edward Arnold, London, 1977), pp. 315–48
Hawkes, Terence. *Structuralism and Semiotics* (Methuen, London, 1977)
Hervey, Sandor. *Semiotic Perspectives* (George Allen & Unwin, London, 1982)
Hewish, Antony. 'Pulsars', *Scientific American*, vol. 219, no. 4, 1968, pp. 25–35

Hobson, Dorothy. *Crossroads* (Methuen, London, 1982)

Holub, Robert C. *Reception Theory* (Methuen, London, 1984)

Hoggart, Richard. *The Uses of Literacy* (Chatto and Windus, London, 1957)

Jameson, Fredric. *The Prison House of Language: A Critical Account of Structuralism and Russian Formalism* (Princeton University Press, Princeton, 1972)

Jaynes, Julian. *The Origin of Consciousness in the Breakdown of the Bicameral Mind* (Penguin, Harmondsworth, 1982)

Kant, Immanuel. *Critique of Pure Reason* (1781), translated by Norman Kemp Smith (Macmillan, London, 1929)

Katz, Elihu. 'Platforms and Windows: Broadcasting's Role in Election Campaigns', in Denis McQuail, (ed.) *Sociology of Mass Communications* (Penguin, Ringwood, Australia, 1972)

Kolers, Paul A. 'Some Formal Characteristics of Pictograms', *American Scientist*, vol. 57, no. 3, 1969, pp. 348–63

Lamberton, D. McL. 'Communication as a discipline: an economist's reflections' in *Science for a Sustainable Society: Communication*, papers given during the 50th Jubilee Congress of ANZAAS 1980 (ANZAAS, Adelaide, 1980), pp. 47–61

Langer, Susanne K. *Philosophy in a New Key* (Harvard University Press, Cambridge, Mass., 1942)

de Lauretis, Teresa. 'Semiosis Unlimited', *PTL: A Journal for Descriptive Poetics and Theory of Literature*, vol. 2, 1977, pp. 367–83

Leach, Edmund. *Lévi-Strauss* (Fontana/Collins, London, 1970)

Lyne, John R. 'Rhetoric and Semiotic in C. S. Peirce', *The Quarterly Journal of Speech*, vol. 66, 1980, pp. 155–68

Mackie, A. M. 'Progress in Learning the Meanings of Symbolic Traffic Signs', *Road Research Laboratory LR 91* (Road Research Laboratory, Crowthorne, 1967)

McLuhan, M. *Understanding Media* (Routledge and Kegan Paul, London, 1964)

McQuail, Denis and Windahl, Sven. *Communication Models* (Longman, New York, 1981)

McQueen, Humphrey. *Australia's Media Monopolies* (Widescope, Victoria, Australia, 1977)

Marx, Karl. *The German Ideology*, quoted in T. B. Bottomere and Maximilien Rubel, *Karl Marx: Selected Writings in Sociology and Social Philosophy* (Penguin, Harmondsworth, 1963)

—— *Thesis on Feuerbach*, quoted in T. B. Bottomere and Maximilien Rubel, *Karl Marx: Selected Writings in Sociology and Social Philosophy* (Penguin, Harmondsworth, 1963)

Morley, David. *The Nationwide Audience: Structure and Decoding* (British Film Institute, London, 1980)

—— 'The *Nationwide* Audience', *Screen Education*, no. 39, Summer 1981, pp. 3–14

—— *Foundations of the Theory of Signs*, vol. 1, no. 2 (University of Chicago Press, Chicago, 1938)

Morris, Charles. *Signs, Language and Behavior* (Prentice Hall, Englewood Cliffs, New Jersey, 1946)

Nightingale, V. 'Media Audiences — Media Products?', *Australian Journal of Cultural Studies*, vol. 2, no. 1, 1984, pp. 23–34

Nordenstreng, K. 'Policy for News Transmission', *Educational Broadcasting Review*, August 1971 (reprinted in D. Mcquail (ed.), *Sociology of Mass Communications*, Penguin, Harmondsworth, 1972, pp. 386–405)

Ogden, C. K. and Richards, I. A. *The Meaning of Meaning* (K. Paul, Trench, Trubner and Co., London, 1923)

Orwell, George. *Animal Farm* (Penguin, Harmondsworth, 1951)
—— *Nineteen Eighty-Four* (Penguin, Harmondsworth, 1964)
O'Sullivan, Tim, Hartley, John, Saunders, Danny, Fiske, John. *Key Concepts in Communication* (Methuen, London, 1983)
Packard, Vance. *The Hidden Persuaders* (Longmans Green, London, 1957)
Parkin, F. *Class Inequality and Political Order* (Paladin, St Albans, 1972)
Peirce, Charles Sanders. *Collected Papers* (Harvard University Press, Cambridge, Mass., 1931–58)
Plato, *The Republic*, translated by Francis Macdonald Cornford (Oxford University Press, Oxford, 1941)
Powell, B., Cunningham, A., Hughes, P., Keating, G., Smith, M. 'The Forgettable News: Two Studies on the Recall of TV News', in Patricia Edgar (ed.), *The News in Focus: the journalism of exception* (Macmillan, Melbourne, 1980), pp. 184–200
Randswell, Joseph. 'Some Leading Ideas of Peirce's Semiotic', *Semiotica*, vol. 19, nos. 3–4, 1977, pp. 157–78
Read, Herbert. *A Concise History of Modern Painting* (Thames and Hudson, London, 1959)
Roberts, Don D. *The Existential Graphs of Charles S. Peirce* (Mouton, The Hague, 1973)
Saussure, Ferdinand de. *Course in General Linguistics* (Fontana/Collins, Glasgow, 1974)
Scholes, Robert. *Semiotics and Interpretation* (Yale University Press, New Haven, 1982)
Schudson, Michael. 'Criticising the critics of advertising: towards a sociological view of marketing', *Media, Culture and Society*, vol. 3, 1981, pp. 3–12
Sebeok, Thomas A. *Zoosemiotics: At the Intersection of Nature and Culture* (Peter de Ridder Press, Lisse, Netherlands, 1975)
Sebeok, Thomas A. *Contributions to the Doctrine of Signs* (Peter de Ridder Press, Netherlands, 1976a)
—— 'Iconicity', *Modern Language Notes*, vol. 91, no. 6, 1976b, pp. 1427–56
Shannon, C. and Weaver, W. *The Mathematical Theory of Communication* (University of Illinois Press, Illinois, 1949)
Sless, David. 'The Application of Behavioural Science to Symbol Design', MSc thesis (Durham University, Durham, 1975)
—— 'Visual Communication and Semiology', *Proceedings of the Conference on Interpersonal and Mass Communications* (Clarendon Press, Sydney, 1977a), pp. 123–36.
—— 'Visual Thinking in Education', *Pivot: A Journal of South Australian Education*, vol. 4, no. 2, 1977b, pp. 4–9; reprinted in *The Educational Magazine*, vol. 35, no. 2, 1978, pp. 2–11
—— *Notes Towards Reformulating the Units of Study in Media Studies*, seminar paper given at Birmingham University, Centre for Contemporary Cultural Studies, 1978
—— 'Testing the Effectiveness of Public Information Symbols', *Proceedings of the 14th Annual Conference of the Ergonomics Society of Australia and New Zealand* (Adelaide University, Adelaide, 1978)
—— *Visual Thinking* (Adelaide University, Adelaide, 1978); reprinted 1980, 1982
—— 'Image design and modification: an experimental project in transforming', *Information Design Journal*, vol. 1, no. 2, 1979, pp. 74–80
—— 'The Photograph as Communication: some thoughts for discussion', *Australian Photography Conference* (Working Papers on Photography, Melbourne, 1980a)
—— 'What is the Meaning of the Message', *Science for a Sustainable Society:*

Communication, papers given during the 50th Jubilee Congress of ANZAAS 1980 (ANZAAS, Adelaide, 1980b), pp. 34–46

—— *Learning and Visual Communication* (Croom Helm, London, 1981a)

—— 'Photographic Meaning: An introduction for teachers', *Working Papers on Photography*, no. 8, 1981b, pp. 7–18

—— 'Semiotics — Survey', *Australian Scan*, nos. 9 and 10, 1980–1, pp. 1–3

—— 'The Future of Graphic Communication'. Address delivered to the Graphic Communication Teachers Association of Victoria Annual General Meeting, November 1981, *Graphic Communication Teachers Association Magazine*, no. 9, March 1982, pp. 9–16; reprinted in *Artefacts*, no. 57, June 1982, pp. 11–15

—— 'What We Make Messages Do', *Communication in Australia: selected papers from the second national conference of the Australian Communication Association*, edited by Ted J. Smith III (Warrnambool Institute Press and Australian Communication Association, Warrnambool, 1983a)

—— 'Discourse, Speculation, and the Media', *Media Information Australia*, no. 28, May 1983b, pp. 16–17

—— 'Communication Studies as Science and Semiosis', paper given at the ACA Conference 1983, *Australian Journal of Communication*, no. 3, January–June 1983c, pp. 13–16

—— 'Communication and the Limits of Knowledge', *Prometheus*, vol. 3, no. 1, 1985, pp. 110–18

—— 'The Design of Government Forms', in *Communication and Government*, edited by T. Smith, G. Osborne and R. Penman (Canberra CAE Press, Canberra, 1986)

—— 'Whose Image?', in *Communication and Government*, edited by T. Smith, G. Osborne and R. Penman (Canberra CAE Press, Canberra, 1986)

—— 'Reading Semiotics', *Information Design Journal* (forthcoming)

—— Campbell, David and Cairney, Peter. *Industrial Safety Symbols and a Multi-cultural Workforce*, a report prepared for the Department of Science and Technology, Commonwealth Government (Flinders University of South Australia, Bedford Park, 1981)

—— and Cairney, Peter. 'Symbol Design and Testing Methodology for Public Information Symbols', *CASSR Technical Paper, no. 3* (CASSR, Flinders University of South Australia, 1979), pp. 1–19

—— and Cairney, Peter. 'Understanding Symbolic Signs: Design Guidelines Based on User Responses', *Ergonomics in Practice*, edited by A. Fisher and R. Croft (17th Annual Conference of the Ergonomics Society of Australia and New Zealand, Sydney, 1980), pp. 51–8

—— and Cairney, Peter. 'Communication Effectiveness of Symbolic Safety Signs With Different User Groups', *Applied Ergonomics*, vol. 13, no. 2, 1982a, pp. 91–7.

—— and Cairney, Peter. 'Evaluating the Understanding of Symbolic Roadside Information Signs, *Australian Road Research*, vol. 12, no. 2, June 1982b, pp. 97–102.

Sperber, Dan. *Rethinking Symbolism* (Cambridge University Press, Melbourne, 1977)

Stankiewicz, Edward. 'E. F. Koerner's *Bibliographia Saussureana*', *Semiotica*, vol. 12, 1974, pp. 171–9

Sturrock, John (ed.) *Structuralism and Since* (Oxford University Press, Oxford, 1979)

Suleiman, Susan R. and Crossman, Inge. (eds.) *The Reader in the Text* (Princeton University Press, New Jersey, 1980)

Tobey, Peter. *Pirating Plants* (Peter W. Tobey, Connecticut, 1975)

Uexkull, Thur von. 'Semiotics and the problem of the observer', *Semiotica*, vol. 48, nos. 3–4, 1984, pp. 187–95

Watson, James D. *The Double Helix* (Weidenfeld and Nicholson, 1968)

Wheeler, J., et. al. *Gravitation* (Freeman, San Francisco, 1973)

Williams, Raymond. *Culture and Society 1780–1950* (Chatto and Windus, London, 1958)

—— *Keywords* (Fontana/Croom Helm, Glasgow, 1976)

Williamson, Judith. *Decoding Advertisements* (Marion Boyars, London, 1978)

Wittgenstein, L. *Philosophical Investigations*, translated by G. E. M. Anscombe (Basil Blackwell, Oxford, 1953)

Wren-Lewis, Justin. 'The encoding/decoding model: criticisms and redevelopments for research on decoding', *Media, Culture and Society*, vol. 5, 1983, pp. 179–97

INDEX